Writing
About
Dance

Wendy R. Oliver, EdD
Providence College

Human Kinetics

Library of Congress Cataloging-in-Publication Data

Oliver, Wendy R., 1953-
  Writing about dance / Wendy R. Oliver.
    p. cm.
  Includes bibliographical references and index.
  ISBN-13: 978-0-7360-7610-4 (soft cover)
  ISBN-10: 0-7360-7610-7 (soft cover)

  1. Dance. I. Title.
  GV1594.O55 2010
  792.8--dc22

                                    2009036251

ISBN-10: 0-7360-7610-7 (print)
ISBN-13: 978-0-7360-7610-4 (print)

The Web addresses cited in this text were current as of September 1, 2009, unless otherwise noted.

Acquisitions Editor: Judy Patterson Wright, PhD; **Developmental Editor:** Amy Stahl; **Assistant Editors:** Rachel Brito and Lauren Morenz; **Copyeditor:** Jan Feeney; **Indexer:** Alisha Jeddeloh; **Permission Manager:** Dalene Reeder; **Graphic Designer:** Nancy Rasmus; **Graphic Artist:** Julie L. Denzer; **Cover Designer:** Keith Blomberg; **Photographer (cover):** Thomas Palmer; **Photo Asset Manager:** Laura Fitch; **Visual Production Assistant:** Joyce Brumfield; **Photo Production Manager:** Jason Allen; **Art Manager:** Kelly Hendren; **Associate Art Manager:** Alan L. Wilborn; **Illustrator:** Tammy Page; figure on page 51 by Patrick Winstanley; **Printer:** Versa Press

Printed in the United States of America   10 9 8 7 6 5 4 3 2

The paper in this book is certified under a sustainable forestry program.

Human Kinetics
Web site: www.HumanKinetics.com

United States: Human Kinetics
P.O. Box 5076
Champaign, IL 61825-5076
800-747-4457
e-mail: humank@hkusa.com

Canada: Human Kinetics
475 Devonshire Road Unit 100
Windsor, ON N8Y 2L5
800-465-7301 (in Canada only)
e-mail: info@hkcanada.com

Europe: Human Kinetics
107 Bradford Road
Stanningley
Leeds LS28 6AT, United Kingdom
+44 (0) 113 255 5665
e-mail: hk@hkeurope.com

Australia: Human Kinetics
57A Price Avenue
Lower Mitcham, South Australia 5062
08 8372 0999
e-mail: info@hkaustralia.com

New Zealand: Human Kinetics
P.O. Box 80
Torrens Park, South Australia 5062
0800 222 062
e-mail: info@hknewzealand.com

E4597

contents

preface

When I first began teaching dance at a small Minnesota college many years ago, I assigned dance critiques and research papers as a part of every course. For dance critiques in particular, students asked, "What should we write about?" and "How should we go about doing this?" I soon discovered that no book or article was available that would answer these questions. Although there were guides like Strunk and White's *The Elements of Style*, there was nothing that specifically addressed writing about dance.

To solve this problem, I began writing down my goals and expectations regarding dance critiques, which I shared with my students. I attended workshops on writing across the curriculum and worked briefly as a dance critic. During my time in graduate school, I chose to delve even more deeply into teaching dance criticism. As part of my research, I sat in on the classes of writing instructors and read research on writing instruction, learning theory, aesthetic education, and dance criticism. I analyzed the styles of some professional critics and encouraged my students to emulate the best aspects of these critics' work. I also assigned dance research papers, dance essays, journals, and reflection papers; as a result, I found myself needing to define what it meant to do excellent work in each case.

During that time, I became convinced that writing, learning, and critical thinking go hand in hand and that the most complete kind of learning in any subject area generally involves writing. As dancers, we understand that to be truly engaged in dance, we must experience the physical act of doing it. Writing, like dancing, is a form of doing that engages us intellectually, visually, and even physically (although in a more limited sense than dancing). Adding writing and dancing together offers an exceptionally well-rounded learning experience that involves many areas of the brain.

In discussing these ideas with colleagues, I found that although most dance instructors were assigning papers, they felt that they did not have the time to devise detailed instructions. Many dance courses are not structured in a way that allows class time for teaching writing. *Writing About Dance* helps both students and teachers with this problem. It brings together the many kinds of writing that can be used in a variety of dance classes—technique, composition, improvisation, dance appreciation, history of dance, choreography, introduction to dance, and dance criticism. This book offers informal writing exercises, such as journal writing, as well as instruction in writing formal dance papers, such as dance critiques and research papers. Students can use this book as a guide for many kinds of dance writing and for general writing information that applies to all academic subjects. Teachers may use it for ideas about ways to incorporate writing in their teaching as well as to guide students' writing.

You may also be interested in exploring the various writing assignments included in chapter 3 of this book that a variety of teachers have created for their students. Some of these are exercises that can be done in class. For instance, if you have class discussions on dance issues or about dance performances, you will probably find that a brief in-class writing exercise preceding the discussion can have a positive effect on the quality of the discussion. Other exercises are to be completed outside of class, such as writing a thoughtful letter to the teacher regarding personal goals in dance technique class.

Although I am no longer teaching at that small college in Minnesota, my current students in Rhode Island still have the same questions about writing assignments. To answer those persistent questions and to provide a practical guide to writing about dance, I wrote this book, which I hope you, too, will find useful. Whether you read it from cover to cover or simply pick out the sections relevant to a particular assignment, this book will challenge you to do your best thinking and writing about dance.

acknowledgments

Many dance critics including Deborah Jowitt and Marcia Siegel have inspired me regarding my own writing as well as in developing my students' writing. At Temple University, Brenda Dixon Gottschild taught me about dance criticism and dance research; Sarah Hilsendager taught me about pedagogy. Penny Hanstein at Columbia helped focus my approach to dance criticism pedagogy and related research. I am indebted to all the dance educators who contributed writing exercises to this volume, and especially to Larry Lavender, who helped me in the earliest stages of developing ideas for the book. Thanks also to editor Judy Patterson Wright for assistance in shaping the content and structure of the book, as well as editors Rachel Brito and Amy Stahl for all their work.

how to use this book

Dance and writing already have an excellent partnership, as evidenced by the many wonderful publications in the dance field. Dance scholarship has grown by leaps and bounds in the last few decades, giving dance depth as a discipline. Integrating dance and writing in the classroom can only help dance to thrive as a field by enabling its students to better articulate the amazing experiences of participating in, observing, and studying the art of dance.

Writing About Dance provides you with instruction on writing about the discipline in many contexts. It addresses several aspects of writing and allows the flexibility to select the readings most appropriate to your courses. Each chapter consists of several short sections that may be used separately or together. This book is a tool for the understanding and practice of writing with the ultimate aim of helping you to become a better writer and thinker.

Organization of This Book

Chapter 1 looks at the connection between writing and learning; it explains the kinds of things that students can expect to learn from the process of each kind of writing. Chapter 2 looks at the writing process and some specific dos and don'ts of writing. Chapter 3 focuses on informal writing, such as journal writing and observation exercises, with sample assignments from a variety of teachers across the United States. Chapter 4 outlines an approach to writing dance critiques. Chapter 5 examines persuasive dance essays, dance reading analysis papers, and dance book reviews. Chapter 6 discusses dance research papers.

Benefits of Informal Writing Exercises

1. Writing is a learning tool. Even five minutes of writing time at the beginning or end of an occasional class can be a learning tool. Some suggestions for in-class writing are found in the first two chapters of the book. If there is no class time available for writing, there are many options for take-home assignments. Here is an excerpt from a student assignment that explains how writing helped her in ballet class:

> I have taken dance classes both as a young child and as an undergraduate, but I think I got much more out of this class than my previous ballet classes—and in a large part I attribute that to the way the writing assignments influenced my full, cognizant participation in the course. Writing about myself as a dancer personalized the class; it allowed me to define what goals I wanted to focus on and brought a new level of awareness to my dancing. (Cooper 2008, student 1)

2. Informal writing stimulates thought without the pressure of a formal paper. The main point of informal writing is to stimulate or improve your thought process, not to create a polished product for the teacher. Many of these exercises increase self-awareness or creativity or provide a preparation for discussion. Informal writing is usually graded on a pass-or-fail basis. Journals, free writing, critical-thinking exercises, creative assignments, creating questions for discussion, and answering questions about readings or videotapes are all examples of writing assignments that could be graded pass or fail.

3. Thoroughly explained informal writing assignments get you started directly on writing. This book is designed for use without extensive instruction from a teacher. The informal writing exercises and formal papers are explained thoroughly so that you can apply the information as you write. While it is always helpful for teachers to share expectations for each assignment, this book offers the flexibility of using assignments that are already laid out and can be used as is or with a teacher's modifications.

The informal writing exercises are offered buffet style so that teachers may select the ones appropriate for the class and amount of time available. At five minutes, the Quick Write exercise in chapter 3 is the shortest option in the book; others take longer, and some are spread out over the entire term. These exercises are organized into three groups: reflection, creative process, and focus on writing. Reflective writing exercises examine some aspect of your own dancing or beliefs related to dancing. Creative process exercises stimulate artistic work and are especially well suited for classes in improvisation or composition. Focus on writing exercises offer practice in description, analysis, and summarizing.

Benefits of Writing Formal Papers

Assignments of papers in the dance class serve many purposes and enhance the teaching of any subject matter. As research on writing has shown, writing deepens learning in a way that discussion alone cannot (Carter et al. 2007; Hilgers et al. 1999; Quitadamo and Kurtz 2007). Writing is also a tangible record of your involvement with assigned subject matter and shows the teacher that some learning has taken place. Both critical thinking and creative thinking are involved in the writing process, with parallels in the process of making dances; these kinds of thinking are important to real-life success and enhance almost any career path that you might take. Finally, good writing is an important skill to have both during the undergraduate years and afterward. Most jobs today involve some form of written communication, so it's a good idea to become a proficient writer before you graduate. In addition to these general reasons for writing about dance, here are some of the specific benefits of writing each formal paper discussed in the book:

Dance Critique

- Gets you out to see dance performances
- Assures the teacher that you have actually attended the event
- Requires careful observation of the performance
- Requires thought and discussion about aesthetic matters, helping to develop your sense of taste
- Develops skills in descriptive and analytical writing

Philosophical Dance Essay

- Gives a sense of dance's connection to the greater world
- Develops argumentation skills
- Introduces you to the idea of dance as a realm for serious discussion of abstract ideas

Editorial Dance Essay

- Gives a sense of dance within contemporary society
- Develops argumentation skills
- Connects you to ideas that might serve as the locus for social, political, or artistic change

Dance Reading Analysis Paper

- Assures the teacher that you have read the material beyond a skimming level
- Prepares you for class discussion
- Familiarizes you with outstanding readings selected by the teacher
- Engages you in critical consideration of historical and contemporary dance issues

Dance Book Review

- Assures the teacher that you have read the material beyond a skimming level
- Prepares you for class discussion or oral presentation
- Familiarizes you with a particular author, artist, or set of concepts deemed important by the teacher
- Develops skills in analysis and evaluation by requiring a supported recommendation

Dance Research Paper

- Increases awareness of dance as an art form that has its own history and theory
- Develops knowledge of a particular topic
- Develops skills in analysis, argumentation, and synthesis
- Develops interest and curiosity about specific aspects of dance

Sample Papers

Included in chapters 4 to 6 are some sample papers that might aid you as you write your own papers. These papers were written by college students who had strong writing skills but little previous experience in writing about dance. Their success at this task serves as a reminder that dance writing is a learnable skill. When reading these papers, keep in mind that each is just one example of a way that a particular type of paper can be written, and yours may take a different approach. These papers are examples of good dance prose; they are not intended to restrict your style.

Evaluation and Rubrics

A rubric is a set of criteria indicating how an assignment will be evaluated. It typically lists specific qualities of papers at the levels of excellent, good, adequate, and poor, although the number of levels may vary. Rubrics are useful because when you know the specific criteria by which papers are graded, you are more likely to do a good job with the assignment. Each of the chapters for formal papers in this book (chapters 4, 5, and 6) includes rubrics that describe expectations for the style and content of the work and may be presented as a list or as a table. Rubrics created for the papers in chapters 4 to 6 were based on rubrics for writing proficiency in Rhode Island and New Hampshire (*Rhode Island and New Hampshire Local Grade Level & Grade Span Expectations for Written and Oral Communication including New England Common Assessment Program, State Grade Level and Grade Span Expectations for Writing* 2006). Each was modified to suit the particular assignment as well as the writing ability of beginning-level undergraduate students.

Some suggestions for students using the rubrics include the following:

- Before you begin your writing process, read the rubric appropriate to the particular kind of paper you plan to write so that you are aware of what elements should be included.
- After you've completed the first draft of your paper, check it against the rubric and incorporate anything that is missing, or strengthen elements that need improvement.

Here are some suggestions for teachers using the rubrics:

- The rubrics in chapters 4 to 6 may be used for evaluation of formal papers. The ratings of excellent, good, adequate, and poor may be translated to number or letter grades as you see fit. If you

xiv   how to use this book

like, you may assign a point value to each area of the rubric: 4 points for excellent, 3 for good, 2 for adequate, and 1 for poor. Total point values can be tallied and ranges assigned a grade. For example, the rubric for dance critiques in chapter 4 has eight elements, so the highest possible number of points that could be earned would be 32 (i.e., 4 multiplied by 8).

- Some people (as I do) prefer a more global approach, using the rubric as a general guideline for grading without using points.
- The rubrics are offered with the intention of being helpful, not restrictive. However, despite good intentions, any list of necessary elements runs the risk of being inadequate, incomplete, or not exactly appropriate. Feel free to modify the criteria so that they reflect your own impression of excellence for each assignment.

Tips for Teachers

This section provides teachers with ideas for implementing the various exercises and assignments discussed in this book. You will also see some antiplagiarism strategies and some suggested reading on writing.

Teaching Suggestions for Informal Writing

The informal writing exercises in chapter 3 are designed to be included in a variety of courses. At the beginning of each writing exercise is a list of the classes for which it is most appropriate. You will also see the objectives for each exercise as well as an overview of what it entails and how long it takes.

As mentioned earlier, the three groups of informal writing exercises are reflection, creative process, and focus on writing. The third group, focus on writing, is particularly helpful as a preparation for writing formal papers: Dancing to Write, Writing to Dance; Observation and Description Exercise; and Dance in a Ritual Context are all excellent practice for writing a good performance critique. The summary paper is a precursor to writing an essay, reading analysis paper, or research paper.

Here are two additional ideas for informal writing assignments based on required readings:

- Students generate their own questions for discussion based on the reading. Questions should promote thoughtful contemplation rather than a quick, factual answer. These may be used for prompting class discussion or simply collected as evidence that the reading has been done.
- Students write answers to specific questions from the teacher about the reading.

Teaching Suggestions for Dance Critique

Another good precursor to writing a critique of a live performance (as discussed in chapter 4), in addition to the writing exercises suggested previously, is to watch a DVD of a single dance work in class and follow up with a guided discussion. This exercise is included in the appendix.

I require students to write one to three dance critiques for every dance course that I teach, including all technique classes, dance history, pedagogy, and dance composition. Critiques are a wonderful way to guarantee that students will attend live performances and think about them critically.

Teaching Suggestions for Dance Essays, Reading Analysis Papers, and Book Reviews

Persuasive essay assignments, such as those in chapter 5, ask students to express an opinion on some aspect of dance that they might not otherwise consider. Since every high school student preparing for college already has considerable practice in writing short essays, a persuasive essay can be a good first writing assignment for a technique class. It allows you to get to know something about each student's opinions and writing style and encourages students to think of dance as a distinct discipline with its own content and controversies.

Reading analysis papers (RAPs) are an excellent way of ensuring that students do in-depth reading of assigned materials. These assignments also encourage students to "converse" with the material by considering whether or not they agree with ideas presented and why. RAPs are an excellent preparation for discussion: When students have carefully thought about ideas in the readings, they are more self-assured about discussing them. RAPs are appropriate in any type of dance class with required reading, whether it is in the studio or in the classroom. I use them in my classes in beginning technique, dance history, and women in dance and sport.

Book reviews are great for a course in which each student is assigned a different book to read. In my class on children's dance (a pedagogy course), each student reads a different instructional book, writes a book review, and makes a brief presentation on it. In a dance history class, students could each select a choreographer's biography to read, review, and report on.

Teaching Suggestions for Dance Research Papers

To promote advance planning and encourage deeper engagement with subject matter, I highly recommend a brief preliminary assignment that is due about two weeks before the finished paper. This causes students to gather their resources and begin reading well in advance of the deadline for the paper. The assignment includes the topic, guiding question, bibliography, and one sentence about the direction of the paper, including names of people or works that might be used as supporting examples, if appropriate to the topic. This allows you to ensure that students have chosen a good topic and have created an interesting guiding question for their research. (See chapter 6 for an explanation.) You will also be able to see if the references they've selected are appropriate for the subject. By writing your comments on the assignment and returning it quickly to students, you will help them get or stay on course.

My suggestion for references is that students be required to use mainly books, journals, magazines, and newspapers, either in hard copy or online. Internet sources such as single-owner Web sites, blogs, and Wikipedia should be prohibited or kept to a minimum. The main reason for this restriction is to make certain that students are using reputable sources for their research that have been checked for accuracy. Students may occasionally need to break this rule, for instance, if their topic requires quoting confessional statements from dancers with an eating disorder, which can be found on personal Web sites. However, using non-refereed sources should be discouraged unless there is a very good reason provided by the student.

I realize that convenience is a big factor in student research and that students will do most of their work from their computers. But I encourage students to actually browse the shelves of their libraries, where they might happen upon materials that they cannot easily find using the online search function. Using online journal, magazine, and newspaper articles is a good supplement to browsing the shelves and using interlibrary loan. I also encourage students to use videos, DVDs, or video clips from the Internet for any topic that requires knowledge of a particular dance style, technique, choreographer, or work. Short movement descriptions can dramatically enhance the effectiveness of discussing specific dances or choreographers.

A Word About Plagiarism

Some colleges and universities, including my own, require a statement about plagiarism on every syllabus. This statement defines plagiarism and states the specific consequences for committing it. Highlighting this statement on the first day of class and then again on the day that a research paper is assigned helps students understand the importance of this issue. Especially because some plagiarism is inadvertently committed in ignorance, students should be educated about what it is and why it is problematic. (See chapter 6, p. 140, for more information.)

While plagiarism can occur in any kind of assignment, it is most common in the writing of research papers. The kind of research assignments that you give to students can reduce the possibility of academic dishonesty. The use of a guiding question along with a topic (discussed in chapter 6) will help make students' research more original. However, some students may be tempted to buy dance papers on the Internet or to copy sentences, paragraphs, or major ideas from sources without attribution.

To deter and detect plagiarism, it is a good idea to use a service such as www.Turnitin.com. This program requires that students upload their papers directly into the Turnitin site, where their papers will be scanned for possible plagiarism. Many colleges and universities have an institutional subscription to these services; contact your teaching technology staff to see if the service is available.

However, some online companies have figured out a way to work around computerized plagiarism-detection systems. These services market papers as "unplagiarized" because they are custom-written to customer specifications and can pass undetected through plagiarism-scanning devices. If students have the money and desire to purchase such a paper, they can. Since no system for plagiarism detection is foolproof, it's a good idea to combine technology and your own best judgment when it comes to detecting plagiarism.

Suggested Reading for Teachers

I have found several books helpful in my own quest to help students become better dance writers. Here are a few of them:

The Elements of Teaching Writing: A Resource for Instructors in All Disciplines, by Katherine Gottschalk and Keith Hjortshoj. Boston: Bedford/St. Martin's Press, 2004.

Engaging Ideas: The Professor's Guide to Integrating Writing, Critical Thinking, and Active Learning in the Classroom, by John Bean. San Francisco: Jossey-Bass, 1996.

A Short Guide to Writing about Art, by Sylvan Barnet, 9th ed. New York: Prentice-Hall, 2007.

Writing about Theatre & Drama, by Suzanne Hudson, 2nd ed. Belmont, CA: Thomson Wadsworth, 2006.

Wrap-Up

Writing About Dance offers both informal and formal writing exercises that are linked to your experiences in dance class. Informal writing includes journal writing, free writing, creative and critical-thinking exercises, and goal setting; this type of writing is usually graded pass or fail. Formal writing includes dance critiques, dance essays, dance reading analysis papers, dance book reviews, and dance research papers; rubrics for these papers help you understand how excellence is defined in each case. Teachers may choose whichever assignments seem the most interesting and appropriate for their classes. Some suggestions for teachers regarding implementation of assignments round out this section of the book.

Writing, Dancing, and Critical Thinking

"Students can't—and don't—learn without writing, panel says" was the headline for a *New York Times* article written by Tamar Lewin on April 26, 2003. The National Commission on Writing in America's Schools and Colleges found that writing "is among the most important skills a student can learn; that it is the mechanism through which students learn to connect the dots in their knowledge" (2003, section A, 15).

But how does writing relate to dance? Obviously, in contrast to the previous statement, students *do* learn to dance without writing. When dancers take a technique class in the studio, they observe the teacher, listen to spoken cues and the music, watch other dancers and themselves, and move in response to that visual and auditory input. Writing is not usually a part of this experience. But what if it were?

The *Times* article—mentioned previously—notes that writing in any discipline deepens your thought process regarding the content you are contemplating. When you write, you engage in critical thinking. You formulate your ideas, put them into words, read them, and reshape them in a continual dialogue with yourself, trying to find and express interesting ideas about dance or yourself. This book offers some answers and comments on the question of ways in which your knowledge of dance might be enhanced through writing.

Depth of Knowledge

Educational researcher Norman Webb and colleagues (2006, 2007) assert four levels of learning: recall, skill or concept, strategic thinking, and extended thinking. Students should experience all four levels of depth of knowledge in order to increase intelligence and develop problem-solving skills for the real world. The higher the level, the more complex its associated activities (Webb 2005).

- Level 1: Recall involves recollection of facts or procedures.
- Level 2: Skill or concept uses information or conceptual knowledge in two or more steps.
- Level 3: Strategic thinking requires reasoning and developing a plan or sequence; it includes activities such as developing a logical argument or drawing conclusions.
- Level 4: Extended thinking requires a long-term problem that you are attempting to solve, with a consideration of multiple solutions.

When writing a dance paper, you use level 3 and level 4 skills, which are particularly beneficial in developing your brain power. For instance, writing a dance research paper involves planning your topic, finding materials, developing a thesis and arguments to support your stance on the topic, synthesizing your information, and drawing conclusions. It is a long-term, multilayered process involving problem solving, as outlined by these kinds of questions: What will I write about? What will my guiding question be? What is the answer to my guiding question? How can I best convey this knowledge to my readers?

Writing Theory

Many years before Webb or the National Commission on Writing published their findings, writing theorists, including Janet Emig, had already published extensively on the position of writing in the curriculum. Emig (1977, 85) noted that higher cognitive functions such as analysis and synthesis "develop most fully only with the support system of verbal language—particularly, it seems, of written language." Psychologists Lev Vygotsky, A.R. Luria, and Jerome Bruner all shared the belief that writing is not only helpful but necessary for provoking some aspects of critical thought.

Jerome Bruner (1996, 1971) offers three ways in which humans represent and organize their experience of the world: enactive, iconic, and symbolic. Enactive refers to doing, or acting on the environment, as in lifting an object. Iconic refers to understanding through pictures or images, as in watching a film. Symbolic refers to comprehending through words, as in talking or writing. In young children, these abilities develop successively. Babies first act on their environment by touching and manipulating objects. Then they learn to recognize pictures of these objects. Finally, they learn the words for them. Bruner maintains that the most effective learning will use more than one of the modes at a time. Emig points out that all three of these modes are used during the writing process: You transform the thought of a word into the symbol for a word (symbolic) as you physically write or type (enactive), which becomes an image on the page (iconic). Similarly in dance, you may transform thoughts or feelings into gestures or movements (symbolic) through use of the body (enactive), which you may see in the mirror or on fellow dancers (iconic). The process of writing is a continual loop among the hand (or body), eye, and brain, and it "marks a uniquely powerful multi-representational mode for learning" (Emig 1977, 88; see figure 1.1).

As a result of the ideas of researchers like Emig, many colleges and universities began to develop writing across the curriculum programs, which were designed to develop students' writing by requiring writing in many subject areas, not just English classes. Another movement called writing in the disciplines also emerged. This variation on writing across the curriculum promoted the idea that students should learn to write in the style of professionals within their major fields.

Many researchers continue to investigate the relationship between writing and learning (Carter et al. 2007, Quitadamo and Kurtz 2007, Ellis and Taylor 2005, Oxbrow 2005, Hilgers et al. 1999, Hodges 1996, Kelly 1995). For instance, in interviews with biology students, Carter and colleagues found that students valued writing lab reports because the reports helped students make the connection between concepts learned in the lecture and the application in the lab. Students experienced synthesis and ordering of information as they wrote lab reports, as well as reflection and interpretation, all of which led to learning. As one student noted, "When you really put it down on paper, you have to put it all together, and somehow it has a way of making you understand everything a lot better. It

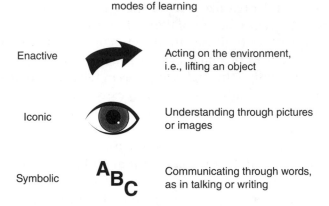

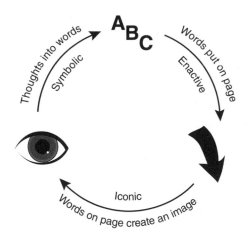

Figure 1.1 The writing process loop.

Adapted from Jerome Bruner, 1971, *The relevance of education* (New York: W.W. Norton & Co.); and from J. Emig, May 1977, "Writing as a mode of learning," *College Composition and Communication* 28:122-28.

forced me to put all my thoughts together instead of having them all jumbled up…" (Carter et al. 2007).

Writing is a cognitive activity that involves setting goals, planning, and organizing ideas. But it is also a creative activity that has much in common with making dances. According to Sharples and

Ransdell (1996, 147), "Writing is creative, and like other creative activities, has no simple goal. It involves the exploration of experience through reflection." This model shows that the writing process starts with a guiding idea or assignment, then cycles through planning, engagement (actual writing), reviewing (reading and interpreting what has been written), and contemplation; the cycle repeats as many times as necessary for revisions and additions (see figure 1.2). Making dances loosely follows this pattern, starting with a choreographic problem (generated either by oneself or a teacher); planning, creating, and performing movement; reviewing what is created; and contemplating or forming new ideas.

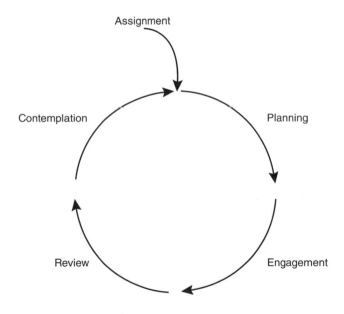

Figure 1.2 The creative process model.

Adapted from M. Sharples, 1996, An account of writing as creative design. In *The science of writing: Theories, methods, individual differences, and applications*, edited by Levy, M. and S. Randsdell (Mahwah, NJ: Lawrence Erlbaum Associates, Inc.).

Writing About Dance

Writing about dance teaches you in two ways simultaneously. First, you learn dance content as you write. In-class writing assignments, journals, creative process papers, dance essays, dance book reviews, and dance research papers in the context of a dance class or course require engaging with dance as a subject. Whether informal or formal, each kind of writing allows you to look at some aspect of dance and become acquainted with it. More formal papers such as essays and research papers demand that you become a momentary expert on the subject at hand.

Second, as noted previously, writing itself is a way of learning. Writing is connective in the way it uses language to state concepts. It can tie things or ideas together, and can record abstract formulations that might otherwise be impossible to grasp. In one study on the effect of talk and writing on learning science, the authors discovered that "analytical writing is an important tool for transforming rudimentary ideas into knowledge that is more coherent and structured" (Rivard & Straw 2000, 566). Writing is an active process that is physically and mentally involving, and requires bringing your personal viewpoint to the page. The critical thinking and contemplation involved in writing can deepen your understanding of dance technique, dance creativity, and dance as an art form.

Writing offers dancers another form of self-expression, one that deepens their understanding of dance.
Philadanco of Philadelphia, Pennsylvania.
Photo by Deborah Boardman.

Informal Writing Exercises

Have you ever been asked to keep a dance journal as an assignment for a technique class? This is an example of an informal writing exercise designed to help you reflect on yourself as a dancer or on some other aspect of class. Reflective exercises offer the opportunity to think about what you are learning, what you are experiencing in your environment, and what you hope to accomplish. Typically in a formal paper you are not asked to share your feelings, impressions, or life experiences; but in reflective writing, all of these things are important.

Another way that informal writing can be useful is by stimulating creativity. In a composition or choreography class, or any class where you need to make a dance, writing can motivate you, chart your progress, clarify your process, and help you plan, just to name a few possibilities. Your writing may be poetic or practical, but in either case, you are getting those brain synapses fired up and primed for creating something unique.

And speaking of unique, the most notable aspect of dance among all the arts is that it moves so much and leaves so little behind: Now you see it, now you don't! How do you write descriptively about an art form that changes from moment to moment? Informal writing exercises can give you practice at this task by asking you to use your powers of observation and a vivid vocabulary to capture specific movements or movement phrases. Sometimes it is also helpful to describe movement from the inside out, that is, from the performer's point of view.

Since teachers usually do not give informal writing a letter grade, you can think of this kind of writing as a chance to experiment. Informal writing is mainly for your own benefit—to help you learn—so use it to your advantage!

Formal Papers

You have just been assigned a dance research paper for one of your courses. What topic should you choose? What kinds of resources should you use? How should your paper be organized? How can you make your paper interesting for the reader and meaningful for yourself?

Chapters 4 to 6 discuss formal papers, including dance critiques or reviews, dance essays, and dance research papers. A dance critique is a thoughtful discussion of a particular dance performance, including an overview of the performance as a whole and some detail on performance highlights. You may critique one evening-length work or a few shorter works. This kind of writing requires an understanding of description, analysis, interpretation, and evaluation and the relationship among them.

A persuasive essay attempts to convince the reader of a particular viewpoint on a given subject. Two kinds of persuasive essays are philosophical and editorial. A philosophical essay examines ideas concerning the nature of dance. For example, what is the difference between dance and an aesthetic sport, such as gymnastics or figure skating? Or, what are some of the functions of dance in our culture today? In your opinion, which of these are most important, and why? An editorial dance essay looks at a particular issue of concern within the contemporary dance world and offers a well-supported opinion or clarifying discussion on that matter. These topics might include the treatment of men in dance, how grant money is dispersed among choreographers, or why dance in the public schools should be federally mandated.

Reading analysis papers and book reviews focus on summary and analysis of reading material. Reading analysis papers typically cover one long reading or a group of short ones; they include a summary of each article as well as an examination of a few key issues within one or more of the readings. Book reviews discuss an entire book and make a recommendation concerning its value to the reader.

Research papers synthesize a variety of information on a given topic in order to bring the reader a new understanding or perspective. It is often helpful to frame a guiding research question that will be investigated during the course of your research. Ultimately, the answers to the research question then become the thesis statement for the paper. When you write an in-depth research paper, you become an expert on your topic and carry that knowledge forward into your life.

Wrap-Up

When you write, you engage in higher cognitive functions such as analysis, synthesis, strategic thinking, and extended thinking. In addition to stimulating your intellectual capabilities, writing is a creative process that is similar to creating a dance. Both start with a guiding idea, then move into planning, engagement (the actual writing or dancing), reviewing, and contemplation; this cycle may be repeated as necessary until you are satisfied with your paper or dance.

Two types of dance writing are informal exercises and formal papers. Informal writing can be done inside or outside of class, and it usually reflects your personal experience with some aspect of dance. Formal papers include dance critiques, dance essays, and dance research papers; these are discussed in more detail in later chapters. Writing in any discipline deepens your thought process regarding the content you are contemplating.

an overhead camera projects their image the live feed of moving dancers projected vertically on the sion. The ground seems

2

The Writing Process

Writing is a creative process similar to choreographing a dance. Both begin with an idea or assignment and then progress to a planning stage, followed by the physical action of writing or dancing. After a period of activity, the writer or choreographer stops to review what has been created so far. A period of contemplation follows, during which the creator makes decisions about the material she has made. Then the cycle repeats, and more material is planned, generated, reviewed, and contemplated. This continues until the creator is satisfied that the work is complete. At some point along the way, another person or group may read or view the work and offer insights or questions that clarify its direction. The creator takes this feedback and uses it to make revisions.

Although the cycle described here is accurate, it is also somewhat vague, and that is a good thing. Writers have different ways of working within this cycle. For some people, the beginning stages of writing a paper might include writing an outline, while others do better without it. The way you approach writing also varies depending on the kind of paper you write. A research paper requires extensive reading before you can even develop a guiding question for your writing. A short essay based on your view of how television has influenced contemporary dance forms might not require any reading at all.

The important thing to keep in mind is that writing is a process rather than a series of steps. To talk about a process, you have to give it some kind of form, but it also needs to be flexible. Writing can be messy and chaotic in the beginning stages. But don't let that scare you, because that is the element of adventure that can actually make writing enjoyable.

If you've ever taken a trip to an unfamiliar place, you have probably had the sensation of being a little unsure about what will happen while you are there. You may have planned an itinerary of places to stay and things to do, but many variables cannot be accounted for in advance, such as lost luggage or running into an old friend who invites you to a wonderful party. The tone and content of your visit will be affected by details such as these. Similarly, when writing a paper, you may have a general plan, but it cannot tell you exactly how you will get from point A to point B. You simply have to start following your plan, pay attention, and see where it leads.

Stages of the Writing Process

When you write, you are not transcribing fully formed paragraphs directly from your brain to the page or computer screen. Instead, your fingers and your brain are working together to produce words, sentences, and paragraphs. With perseverance, this partnership will eventually result in a finished paper. What follows is an overview of the writer's process and some tips for good writing; more specific guidelines for writing each type of paper are included in later chapters. This process follows the model shown in figure 1.2 in chapter 1.

PLANNING ➤ Assignment and Planning

Your teacher gives you an assignment: Go see a live dance performance and write a critique. The *planning*, or preparation, part of the cycle involves reading up about the company or kind of dance you will see, going to the performance, taking notes, and reflecting on what you saw. Or perhaps your assignment is to write an essay about a current issue in dance, such as the lack of funding for arts in public schools, or the popularity of ballroom dance on college campuses. In this case, you might do some reading, but much of your preparation will revolve around developing a guiding question that will prompt your writing. If your assignment is a research paper, your preparation is a lengthy process involving reading, note taking, organizing, and developing a guiding question. A good research paper takes a lot of preparatory work before the drafting of the paper begins; in fact, some experts (Thaiss and Davis 1999) say that about 80 percent of your time in writing a research paper will be preparation.

Whichever kind of paper you are preparing to write, if it involves reading, then excellent note taking is important.

Tips for Taking Notes While Reading

1. For every source you use, be sure to get all bibliographic information.

   - For books: author, title, publication date, publisher, and place of publication.
   - For articles: author, title of article, name of journal, volume, issue number, and page numbers or articles.
   - Web sites: author, title of article, title of the page, title or owner of the site, URL, and date accessed.

   Nothing is more annoying than realizing that you are missing some vital piece of information about a book or article that you used and no longer have available when it comes time to write up your reference list.

2. Take the time to summarize each article or chapter you read. That will ensure that you understand what you have read and that you have expressed it in your own words. If you are reading entire books, skim them, looking for chapters most pertinent to your topic, and focus on those. Or if reading the entire book thoroughly is important to your research, summarize the entire book.

3. Write down questions, comments, and concerns that occur to you as you read. Is there something that you don't understand? A new interpretation of an old theme or idea? Jot it down. Do you see a connection between this article and the one you read earlier? Make a note of it.

4. Write down useful quotations, and be sure to include the page numbers. When you write your paper, you will probably need some quotations, but don't go overboard. Even a research paper should be only about 20 percent quotations, or less.

When taking notes at a performance, such as this one by Andalucia Flamenco Ballet of Spain, focus on vivid description.

© FETHI BELAID/AFP/Getty Images

Note taking is also vital in the preparation stages of writing a dance critique. Good note taking is the raw data that all of your observations and analysis will be built on. If the raw data is incomplete or garbled, it will be difficult to write a good paper.

Tips for Taking Notes at a Performance

1. Bring a large notebook and pen. Read the entire program before the show begins so that you'll know the number of dances and when intermissions will happen.

2. Number each dance on your program, and put a corresponding number on the top of the page of notes so that you can remember which notes go with which dance.

3. Since you will be in the dark for the duration of most indoor performances, it's a good idea to practice writing in the dark, or you can create a similar effect by writing with your eyes closed.

4. An alternative to writing in the dark is writing between dances when the lights come up, or writing during intermission and immediately after the show. However, writing as the dance unfolds usually yields the greatest amount of detail, and detail is crucial to excellent critiques.

5. If you are writing in the dark, try keeping the index finger of your nonwriting hand in place at the start of the line where you are writing. When you reach the end of the page, return to this finger, move the finger down a bit, and begin writing again. This may help you avoid the problem of writing on top of what you have already written. Avoid the temptation to use your cell phone light or a laptop computer, because that disturbs those around you. Keep your electronic devices off and stowed away.

6. If you are writing about an outdoor performance, or one in a nontraditional performing space, be sure to include a brief description of the environment.

7. Write down details, including number of men, number of women, color and type of costume, type of music, and general movement style. Note different sections in the dance, and be sure to write down some specific movements that you see, even if you don't know their names (just describe them).

8. Remember to bring your program home with you. It will provide you with important information as you write your critique.

Organizing

Another element of preparation is organizing your information. If you have taken notes, you'll want to put them in some kind of order that makes sense to you. For instance, for a research paper, you might group together notes about particular people or subtopics, or you might think of large points that you want to make and which sources support which points. If you were writing a research paper on the development of *The Nutcracker* over time, you would likely have information about various productions of the ballet that have been done in the past. You could organize these notes chronologically, by ballet company, by choreographer, or in another way that seems logical. You might find an outline useful at this stage of your preparation. By all means, refer to a book on editorial style for more information on outlining, such as *The Little, Brown Handbook* (Fowler and Aaron 2007), *The Elements of Style* (Strunk and White 2008), or the *Chicago Manual of Style* (2003).

Developing the Guiding Question or Assignment

For some types of papers such as dance critiques, summaries, or reading analysis papers, your focus is predetermined by the assignment. However, for an essay or research paper, you will need to find a guiding question that focuses your inquiry and gives direction to your paper. Developing this question is actually a way of narrowing your topic. This question may occur to you right at the beginning of your process, or you may need to wait until after you've done all your reading and even some of your writing before you find the right question. Your contemplation or research on the guiding question should eventually lead you to an answer, which will then become the basis for your thesis, which is the main assertion in your paper. The chapters on essays and research papers later in this book discuss this process in more detail.

ENGAGEMENT ➤ Engagement: Free Writing—Round 1

In the writing process model, the actual act of writing is termed *engagement*, since it is this aspect of the process where you are actually engaged in the physical activity of writing or typing. Some people like to outline the entire paper before they begin writing, but I am not one of them. If you do like to outline, by all means do so. If not, I recommend free writing. Free writing, a term popularized by writing teacher Peter Elbow (1998), means to write in a stream-of-consciousness way, without self-judgment, usually for a short period (10 to 20 minutes), but possibly for much longer. The idea is to allow yourself to write without worrying about logic, grammar, flow, or sentence construction.

Your job is to write as much as you can in response to the guiding question that you posed for yourself. Write without censoring yourself, and concentrate on articulation of your ideas. Do not refer to your notes or use quotations at this point; the focus should be on the understanding you bring to your subject based on the preparation that you have done so far. If you get stuck, digress to a related topic and keep writing. Aim for a minimum of 10 minutes. Free writing can feel chaotic because it doesn't have a planned outcome. Although you don't know what the result will be, continue writing to the best of your ability.

REVIEW ➤ Reviewing

The next stage of this process is *reviewing*, as in rereading what you have written so far. When you finish your 10 minutes or so of free writing, take time to carefully read through what you have and look for ideas that can serve as the basis for further discussion and exploration. You could pull one of these ideas out and do another free write, or you could take the most important point you've made and use that as the core of your paper. The ultimate goal of your free write is to find one or more main points for your paper and to begin to analyze all the information that you have gathered in your preparation stage. Because you are doing this on your own, without reference to notes or books, it will necessarily be original work.

Reviewing your writing is necessary in order to appraise it—to see if it makes sense, if it makes the points you want it to make, and if it needs additions. You may find yourself alternating frequently between reviewing and engagement (or reading your work and writing it). There is no hard-and-fast rule about doing everything in a particular order, so do what seems natural for you.

CONTEMPLATION ➤ Contemplation

Here, the cycle starts again. Now is the time to refer to notes and see if there is any specific information that would be important to include. This is also the right time to find quotations that support the points you are trying to make, if this is a paper with references. You will also need to take a look at how well your writing communicates to others and think of ways to improve it.

ENGAGEMENT ➤ Engagement: Free Writing—Round 2

Make the changes and additions that you have considered. Move from your loosely structured free-writing style toward a more standard style designed to communicate with your audience. Rearrange information to improve the flow of your paper, and be sure to include an introduction, body, and conclusion. At the end of this round, you should have your rough draft.

REVIEW ➤ Reviewing by Others

If possible, this is a good time to have a peer or instructor take a look at your writing and offer suggestions. It is helpful to ask your reader specific questions before he or she reads your paper:

- Do all my points make sense?
- Does anything seem unnecessary?
- Does anything need more explanation?
- Can you point out my thesis? Have I supported it adequately?
- Does the paper hold your attention? If not, where is the problem?
- Does each sentence follow logically to the next?
- Are there any grammatical errors?

For each type of paper in this book, there is a checklist that you may share with reviewers in order to help them give you feedback.

One way of providing feedback is to have the reviewer read your paper out loud to you. The reader should pause at any point where the meaning is unclear and ask for clarification. Hearing your own words read aloud will help you to understand how they appear to others and will point out flaws that you may have overlooked. After hearing the paper aloud, ask your reviewer specific questions such as the ones listed previously, and listen carefully to the answers.

Take notes on the feedback, thank your reader, and then do your next round of revising. If it is not possible to have someone else read your paper, then you will need to serve as your own critic. Ask yourself the previous questions, and use checklists provided in the rest of this book. Take time to review your own writing again after the revision, and also check your work against the rubrics provided at the end of chapters 4, 5, and 6.

General Writing Suggestions

Some aspects of writing apply to all kinds of dance papers: audience; tone; structure, coherence, and flow; word choice; punctuation; and syntax.

Audience

Before you can begin to shape your paper, you need to know why and for whom you are writing. Why are you writing this paper? The most obvious reason is that your instructor assigned it to you. However, teachers do not assign papers simply to make students miserable! Writing about dance is a way to solidify your perceptions and opinions of it and to integrate what you may have learned through reading, lectures, films, photographs, or technique classes. All of the avenues through which you have absorbed information about dance merge in the process of writing.

To make dance writing especially meaningful, you need to imagine an audience outside of yourself to whom you can direct your thoughts. Since a teacher assigns and reads your papers, does that make him or her your audience? No. It is better to think of your teacher as your editor rather than your audience. Just as the dance journalist has an editor who scrutinizes all writing before it goes into publication, you have your teacher to give you feedback about how well your writing serves its purpose.

Unless your teacher tells you otherwise, think of your audience as your peers—your classmates. The act of writing is a way for you to share your vision and knowledge with your audience. Knowing your audience helps you to determine what kinds of information to include in your paper and what can be left out. What assumptions can you make about the dance knowledge of your classmates? You can probably assume that your classmates are familiar with basic dance terminology. You may also assume that they have a working knowledge of various dance genres and styles; however, you would probably not assume that they know the background of a particular choreographer, dance, or dance scholar. So while there is no need to define the terms *modern dance* or *jazz dance* for your audience, you might want to mention a program note, written by the choreographer, about how a certain dance came to be. When critiquing a dance performance, assume that your readers have not seen it.

Just like the art of dancing, the act of writing is a way for you to share your vision and knowledge with your audience.

From DanceAbility, Eugene, Oregon.
Photo by Brian Lanker.

In the case of a persuasive essay or research paper, be sure to give a context for your discussion as well as a little background information on any specific artists, genres, or works. Define any terms that would be unfamiliar to your classmates and avoid unnecessary technical language.

Tone

The tone of your paper is the degree of its formality or informality. Informal writing exercises such as free writing may be written in any way that seems natural. For a formal paper, however, you must choose your language more carefully. In general, avoid words that are too casual, including slang such as *awesome, great,* or *sick.* Use proper grammar, and remember that you are the authority for this paper, so speak with assurance.

Even in a formal paper, there are varying degrees of formality. For instance, some dance reviewers write in the first person, while others write in third person. Either voice is correct, although first person is less formal.

First person: "It's wonderful to see Abi Stafford—looking bolder and fresher than I've ever seen her—being given assists by Amar Ramasar and Andrew Veyette, her partners in the first trio" (Jowitt 2008, 1).

Third person: "After much anticipation, Mark Morris' 'Mozart Dances,' set to three of the grand master's piano concertos, opened in Berkeley Thursday in a Cal Performances presentation" (Vasilyuk 2007, 1).

In addition to using first person in dance critiques or reviews, writers may use first person in some kinds of essays, including editorial essays, reading analysis papers, and book reviews, although third person is more common. However, the traditional research paper uses only third person.

Structure, Coherence, and Flow

Structure is the organizational format of a paper, coherence is how it holds together as a whole, and flow is how it moves logically from one thought to the next. Papers that lack one or more of these elements will likely be disorganized and difficult to follow.

The structure of any paper will have an introduction, a body, and a conclusion. The introduction gives a context for your topic, relays something interesting about your topic, and presents your thesis statement. It gives your reader a sense of what you are attempting to analyze, explain, or prove during the course of your paper. The body of your paper conveys its main content; each point is contained in one or more well-organized paragraphs.

In a well-written paper, the topic, thesis, and each paragraph within the body all work together. Each paragraph flows logically to the next, and the conclusion ties the paper together and offers a new insight. In a shorter paper, the conclusion is only one paragraph; in a longer paper, it might be several paragraphs. The reader should experience the coherence and unity of the paper after reading the conclusion. Readers should finish with a deeper understanding of and appreciation for your topic.

Qualities of a Good Paragraph

A good paragraph has a strong topic sentence, usually the first sentence, which states the main idea. The topic sentence gives a paragraph coherence; all the other sentences in the paragraph will relate to the topic sentence, and each sentence will lead logically to the next. A paragraph should be neither too short nor too long, generally five to eight sentences, although there may be exceptions if there is a good reason. If you have typed an entire page of text without hitting your "return" key, your paragraph is too long; you need to go back and find a place to put a break. The end of the paragraph should signal the end of a train of thought, allowing a short pause for the reader to absorb the material before beginning anew with the next paragraph.

Here is an example of a unified paragraph from the body of an article titled "Foundations of Hip-Hop Dance," by Jorge Fabel Pabon (2008). The first sentence, which is also the topic sentence, tells us that the topic will be the beginnings of hip-hop culture. Each sentence connects to that topic, and even more specifically to the idea of naming the movement itself and its dance forms. In addition, this paragraph has good flow, because each idea leads logically to the next.

> In the early 1970s, the unnamed culture known today as hip-hop formed in New York City's ghettos. DJ Afrika Bambaataa named the dynamic urban movement hip-hop in the early 1980s. Certain slang words also became titles of the dance forms, such as rockin' and breakin', generally to describe actions with great intensity. The term "break" was often used as a response to an insult or reprimand, for example, "Why are you breakin' on me?" The break was also the section of a musical recording where the percussive rhythms were most aggressive and hard driving. Dancers anticipated and reacted to these breaks with their most impressive steps and moves. (Fabel Pabon 2008, 59)

Word Choice

A word about words: Selecting the right one for a sentence makes a big difference. You need to be meticulous about words for a few reasons. First, it's important to choose words that convey your meaning as clearly as possible so that readers understand your writing readily as their eyes move down the page. Any vagueness or awkward wording will cause readers to pause and momentarily lose track of what you are saying. Second, many poor word choices are grammatical errors and will be noted by your teacher and other readers as a weakness. In our culture, using good grammar is a sign of being well educated. The conventions of English grammar are not always easy to master, but you must strive toward perfection in this area if you want others to judge your work in a positive light. The final reason to pay attention to word choice is that some wordings are more compelling than others and carry a sense of authority and strength. If you want readers to respect and appreciate what you say, you should phrase your statement in the best possible way. Following are some common concerns related to word choice in your writing.

•   **Active voice:** Use of the active voice energizes your writing and helps keep it concise. By contrast, using the passive voice tends to be wordy and remove the reader from the action. To construct a sentence with active voice, make sure that the subject of the verb is taking the action. Here's an example:

> Active: The choreographer **chose** a compatible designer for his project.

> Passive: A compatible designer **was chosen** by the choreographer for his project.

•   **Subject–verb agreement:** Most people realize that a singular subject requires the use of a singular form of the verb. Here's an example: Fred Astaire was a famous dancer and movie star.
However, when the subject and verb are separated by a long phrase, it is easy to make a mistake.

> Incorrect: A large group of dancers, choreographers, and musicians **collaborate** frequently on projects.

> Correct: A large **group** of dancers, choreographers, and musicians **collaborates** frequently on projects. The verb should be **collaborates** in order to agree with the singular subject (group).

•   **Pronoun–antecedent agreement:** A pronoun such as *he*, *she*, or *they* must agree with the noun to which it refers (known as its antecedent).

Correct: **Ginger Rogers and Fred Astaire** were partners for a long period during **their** careers. (Antecedent is plural, as is the pronoun.)

Incorrect: **Every dancer** has **their** stylistic preferences. Since *every dancer* is singular, the pronoun following it should also be singular.

Correct: **Every dancer** has **his or her** stylistic preferences. If you prefer, you can avoid using *his or her* by making the subject plural: Correct: **All dancers** have **their** stylistic preferences.

Quick Guide to Punctuation

Learning the proper use of the comma, period, colon, and semicolon can save a lot of time and red ink. We often tend to think of punctuation as an add-on to writing, which is not part of the writing itself, but this is a misconception. Punctuation is essential to the core meaning of every sentence; it can make your paragraphs crystal clear or very garbled. Following are some explanations of common punctuation problems and their solutions. For a more complete look at punctuation, see a style guide such as *The Little, Brown Handbook* (Fowler and Aaron 2007), *The Elements of Style* (Strunk and White 2008), or *Chicago Manual of Style* (2003).

Comma

Here are some specific uses of the comma:

- **Between items in a series:** Battement, tendu, pirouette, and glissade are all ballet terms.
- **After introductory words or phrases:** On June 19, 2009, the dancer gave her first performance.
- **Interrupting clauses:** A good place to perform dance, if at all possible, is in a well-equipped theater.
- **Setting off descriptive (appositive) phrases:** Movement quality, or dynamics, is how the movement is performed.
- **Between two independent clauses separated by a conjunction:** The success of our dance company seems assured, but we might be wrong.

A common problem with commas is that they are either underused or overused. One guideline is that a comma should be inserted in a sentence where you would pause if reading aloud. But use caution when following that rule: Some writers insert a comma after a long subject, but that's not correct because the subject and verb should not be separated by a comma. Here's an example of an erroneous use of a comma after a long subject:

Any person not professionally engaged in health, physical education, recreation, dance, or athletics who supports these areas, may become a nonvoting member of our organization. That comma before *may* is incorrect. And writers often erroneously use commas to separate an independent clause from a subordinating clause, as is done here:

Compound-complex sentences include two or more main clauses, and one or more subordinate clauses. Granted, there is a natural pause after the word *clauses,* but a comma should not be used there because the clause that follows the *and* cannot stand on its own. Commas are used to make word groupings within a sentence that aid comprehension. If there are not enough commas, it can be confusing. On the other hand, if there are too many commas, it can slow down the reading unnecessarily and also create problems with clarity.

Other uses of the comma can be found in a style book, but most of them we understand intuitively through our use of spoken language. If you want to check your comma use, have a friend read your paragraph or sentence out loud to you, exactly as you've punctuated it, and see if it makes sense.

Here is a sentence that needs a few commas and some other edits, followed by a corrected version:

> Incorrect: New York New York is often called the "dance capital of the world" but many other cities such as San Francisco and London also have thriving dance communities.

> Correct: New York, New York, is often called the "dance capital of the world," but many other cities, such as San Francisco and London, also have thriving dance communities.

Here is another example:

> Incorrect: At 18 dance students may already be performing professionally.

> Correct: At 18, dance students may already be perform-
> ing professionally.

Comma Splice

One of the most common punctuation errors is the comma splice (also called a run-on sentence), which occurs when two complete sentences (containing both a subject and a verb) are linked with a comma, as in the following example:

> Incorrect: Tap dancer and choreographer Ann Miller became famous in the 1930s, she was recorded in *Ripley's Believe It or Not* as the world's fastest tap dancer at 500 taps per minute.

Instead of using a comma in that spot, writers should chose a period, a semicolon, or a conjunction (such as *and, or, but, since, although*). Each of these is grammatically correct, although one may be preferable to another depending on how closely you choose to link the sections. Here is a rewrite using a semicolon:

> Correct: Tap dancer and choreographer Ann Miller became famous in the 1930s; she was recorded in *Ripley's Believe It or Not* as the world's fastest tap dancer at 500 taps per minute.

See the following section for more information on the use of the semicolon.

Semicolon

As noted earlier, a semicolon joins two complete sentences that are related to each other. The phrases on each side of the semicolon need a subject and a verb; each should be able to stand on its own as a sentence. Usually, the thoughts on either side of the semicolon are of equal importance.

> Square dancing involves four pairs of dancers who stand in a square formation; a live caller tells the dancers what to do as they dance.

Colon

A colon should be used when the words following the colon somehow describe, modify, or summarize the words occurring before the colon.

> Dance serves many functions in our society: artistic, entertainment, social, religious, and cultural, to name a few.

A colon is also used before a list or a series, to introduce a quotation, or in a statement introduced by *the following* or *as follows*.

In this next example, the clause before the colon is modified or explained by the clause that follows the colon. Although the clause before a colon must be a complete sentence, the one after the colon does not need to be complete, although it could be.

> Doris Humphrey built her modern dance technique on the concept of fall and recovery: She believed that dance occurs in the moments between releasing the body into free flow and rising to recover balance.

Quotation Marks and Punctuation

Quotation marks are used to indicate words written or spoken by someone other than the author.

> "You have to love dancing to stick to it."(Merce Cunningham in Brown et al. 1998, 90)

Quotation marks are also used around some titles, such as titles of dances, journal or magazine articles, and song titles. When should dance titles be italicized, and when should they be in quotation marks? The general rule is that the title of an entire concert, performance, or major work is italicized, but the sections within that whole are in quotation marks.

> *University Winter Dance Concert*, "Etude" (where "Etude" is one of several pieces in the show)

> *The Nutcracker*, "Dance of the Sugar Plum Fairy" (where "Dance of the Sugar Plum Fairy" is one of several individual dances within the ballet)

Punctuation in relation to quotation marks can be confusing. Remember that commas and periods *always* go inside quotation marks. Question marks and exclamation marks go inside quotation marks when those punctuation elements are part of the quoted text, but semicolons, colons, and dashes go outside quotation marks.

Three of the dances at the David Parsons concert were "Caught," "The Envelope," and "Fine Dining." Parsons' choreography has been called "witty" and "intelligent"; it can also be intense and serious at times.

Syntax

Syntax, or sentence structure, is important both for reasons of content and style. A sentence that is disorganized or overly wordy can interfere with the reader's comprehension of the message. Variety in syntax is important in creating an interesting and readable style. Familiarize yourself with compound and complex sentences, the use of the colon and semicolon, and basic grammar.

Vary the length of your sentences. The same sentence may be ordered in different ways; each kind of organization has a unique effect on the feeling of your writing. There is not any one kind of syntax that is always preferable to another. The important thing is to use a variety of organizing patterns in your sentences. All of the examples here are taken from dance critiques; however, the same idea also applies in any other kind of paper. Here are four good ways of writing the same idea, each of which uses a different sentence structure:

1. The performance was far too long and I eventually began to lose interest; however, it did include a few delightful pieces.

2. Eventually, I began to lose interest in the performance because it was far too long; however, it did include a few delightful pieces.

3. Although the performance did include a few delightful pieces, it was so long that eventually I began to lose interest.

4. Eventually, I began to lose interest in the performance because it was far too long. However, it did include a few delightful pieces.

Here is a problematic passage that has unvaried syntax; each sentence begins with a noun, then a verb. The sentence length is consistently short, and the punctuation is the same throughout, creating a choppy and uninteresting writing style.

> The music for the dance was by Chopin. There were six female dancers. The dancers wore long, blue dresses. The dancers circled the stage gracefully. They then created many interesting spatial patterns.

A better version of that paragraph is to combine the sentences, creating more flow in the writing:

> Accompanied by the music of Chopin, six female dancers in long, blue dresses circled the stage gracefully and then created many interesting spatial patterns.

In general, try interspersing compound and complex sentences with simpler ones, also paying attention to sentence length and punctuation.

Compound sentences consist of two or more independent clauses (an independent clause is a group of words that can stand alone as a simple sentence or can be connected to other clauses) joined in one of three ways:

1. With a conjunction (*and, but, or, nor, for, so, yet*) and a comma

   > The man rolled slowly across the floor (first clause), and the woman ran swiftly in a circle around him (second clause).

2. With a semicolon

   > As I watched this performance, the partnering reminded me of pairs figure skating; the lifts seemed smooth and effortless.

3. With a semicolon and a conjunctive adverb (*besides, consequently, however, indeed, therefore*)

   > The jazzy quality of this dance was due mainly to the use of hip isolations; however, there were many balletic elements as well.

Complex sentences contain one main clause (or simple sentence) and one or more subordinate clauses, marked by a subordinating conjunction (*after, although, as if, because, if, when, while*) or a relative pronoun (*which, that, what, whatever, who, whom, whoever, whomever*):

> The dancers burst onstage (main clause) when the drummers began to play (subordinating clause).

> It seemed as though the choreographer had created the movement especially for these two dancers because it displayed their abilities so well.

> The women who were left onstage seemed to melt into the background.

Compound-complex sentences include two or more main clauses plus one or more subordinate clauses:

> All of the dancers wearing blue began to accelerate as they danced; however, those in red maintained a constant tempo.

> Even though this dance company has a national reputation, they had technical problems with lights and sound, and the performance was marred as a result.

Spell Check

Spell check is a useful feature on your computer, but it is not infallible. Its main weakness is homophones (words that sound alike but are spelled differently, such as *their* and *there*). Spell check doesn't know the difference if you've used the wrong one, and that also goes for *it's* and *its*; *here* and *hear*; *site, sight,* and *cite*; and many others. Also, words that are similar, such as *loose* and *lose*, will not be flagged by spell check, since they are both legitimate words spelled properly.

Spelling errors make your work look sloppy even if your reasoning is impeccable, so take the extra time you need to proofread. The moral of the story here is to check your spelling by hand in addition to (or instead of) using spell check.

Gender Inclusiveness

The use of the word *man* in a generic way is no longer an acceptable use of language. The ambiguity of the term is troublesome and contradictory: On one hand, *man* means all people, male and female; on the other hand, *man* means all people excluding female persons (men only). Although *man* is supposed to represent all of humanity, it does not. In their book *Words and Women*, Casey Miller and Kate Swift (1976) cite studies in which children and adults demonstrated how deep-seated the "generic man" problem is by showing time and again that many people understand "early man," "political man," "urban man," and the like to indicate the male of the species only. Likewise, the use of the pronoun *he* or *his* to indicate both sexes is misleading.

Fortunately, there are alternatives to the use of *man* for all contexts. The words *people* and *humans* work very well in place of the generic *man*. *He or she* and alternating between the two pronouns are also acceptable alternatives to the generic *he* and *him*. Ideas can often be written in the plural instead of singular, thus avoiding the pronoun problem altogether: *All dancers have unique ways of moving* instead of *Each dancer has his own unique way of moving*. Here are some examples of sexist and nonsexist language:

Man has danced since the beginning of time.	Sexist
People have danced since the beginning of time.	Nonsexist
Men and women have danced since the beginning of time.	Nonsexist
Humans have danced since the beginning of time.	Nonsexist
Every dancer has his own style of moving.	Sexist
Every dancer has his or her own style of moving.	Nonsexist
All dancers have unique ways of moving.	Nonsexist
Each dancer has a unique way of moving.	Nonsexist

Writing in a nonsexist way requires a bit of thought and adaptation, but once the habit is begun, it is not difficult. Many writing guides, including the *Publication Manual of the American Psychological Association* (2009) and *Chicago Manual of Style* (2003), now have chapters or sections on writing with bias-free language.

Wrap-Up

The process of writing papers follows the creative process model described by Sharples, shown in figure 1.2: guiding question or assignment, planning, engagement, reviewing, and contemplation. Planning may involve reading, dancing, or watching dance, depending on the assignment; it generally involves note taking as well. Then you organize the notes and ideas. If the assignment is a research paper or essay, you will need to develop a guiding question. Next comes engagement, or the actual writing of the paper, followed by reviewing, where you reread what you write. That is followed by contemplation, a time to think about additions and changes, which leads to actually making those changes in your second round of engagement. A second period of review, preferably by someone other than you, leads to the final draft of your paper.

General writing suggestions in this chapter include a consideration of your audience; tone; structure, coherence, and flow; word choice; punctuation; syntax, spell check, and gender-inclusive language.

3

Informal Writing Exercises

This collection of writing exercises for dance classes comes from dance educators all over the United States who have found writing a valuable addition to their curriculum. Some of these exercises can be done in class, while others require time outside of class. Most of them are informal, in the sense that they do not result in a formal paper; the focus is on learning through the writing process rather than on the final product.

Like dance improvisation, informal dance writing may include an element of playfulness or risk taking that may not be possible when writing a more traditional, formal paper. Enjoy this opportunity to try your hand at writing expressively, creatively, and descriptively!

The exercises are arranged in three loose groupings: reflection, creative process, and focus on writing.

1. The *reflection* exercises focus on students' individual experiences with dance and their thoughts about those experiences.

2. The *creative process* section includes ideas for stimulating creativity or clarifying the creative process through writing.

3. The *focus on writing* section addresses the nature of writing, how you do it, and how you might do it better within the context of a dance course. The last two exercises in this section result in short, formal papers that could be graded.

Reflection Exercises

A reflection exercise offers you the opportunity to think about dance in a personal way. Whether you are reflecting on your own dancing, the dancing of classmates, or other kinds of dance experiences, you are contemplating what you see or experience in order to understand it more fully. Many reflective exercises will help you grow as a dancer and as a person. These exercises may ask for observations about yourself or others or challenge you to clarify your dance goals and philosophy.

Statements of Personal Goals
Elizabeth Cooper

Class: Any beginning, intermediate, or advanced technique class

Objectives: To learn to identify one's strengths and challenges; to use this information to set personal goals for technical and artistic development

Overview: Three short written reflections over the quarter or semester

These assignments will help you reflect on your strengths and weaknesses as a dancer and will also provide your teacher with useful information, including your dance background, expectations, attitudes toward dance, and reasons for enrolling in the course.

Statement of Course Goals

In one to two pages, please discuss your dance background and the reasons you are taking this course. Identify your strengths as well as your personal challenges in relation to dance. In particular, explain what you hope to accomplish in this class—your personal goals. Finally, please lay out a strategy for achieving your personal goals.

Identification of Alignment and Anatomical Issues

As we begin the term, please give some thought to identifying alignment or anatomical issues that you wish to focus on. In a one-page paper, discuss these issues and develop a strategy using imagery to help correct the problems. I will ask you to revisit this assignment later in the quarter and to write a follow-up analysis.

Teacher's note: I suggest that students consult Valerie Grieg's *Inside Ballet Technique*. I will also bring a skeleton to class to identify particular aspects of the spine, pelvis, hip joint, and scapula.

Postmidterm Self-Assessment

For this one- to two-page assignment, I would like you to reflect on the previous two writing assignments (statement of course goals and the identification of alignment and anatomical issues). For those assignments, you wrote about your strengths as well as your challenges, identified an alignment issue you wished to focus on, and devised an imagistic strategy for correcting the issue. Now that we are more than halfway through the quarter, how do you think you are meeting the technical and artistic challenges you discussed previously? Has your imagery helped in guiding you toward an alignment that supports more efficient dancing? What satisfactions or frustrations do you have? What sort of additional feedback, readings, or classroom work could help you meet these challenges?

Following are two excerpts from student papers for this writing exercise:

> Excerpt of student paper 1: I have taken dance classes both as a young child and as an undergraduate, but I think I got much more out of this class than my previous ballet classes—and in a large part I attribute that to the way these writing assignments influenced my full cognizant participation in the course. Writing about myself as a dancer personalized the class; it allowed me to define what goals I wanted to focus on and it brought a new level of awareness to my dancing.

> Excerpt of student paper 2: I believe that the writing assignments in class have been helpful to my learning. Normally in dance class we don't do writing assignments or identification of goals, so we don't have a focus each day in technique class. With these assignments, I felt that each day I had something to think about. I also think that having us create our own goals made it a more active learning environment. I felt it was my responsibility to make these goals happen and to keep track of my process.

Teacher's note: This assignment is given approximately three to four weeks before the end of the term. The final question in the assignment helps me to identify what additional information I need to address or readdress in the classroom.

Elizabeth Cooper, MFA, teaches at the University of Washington in Seattle.
From W. Oliver, 2010, *Writing About Dance* (Champaign, IL: Human Kinetics).

Self-Reflection Letters

*Cornish College of the Arts dance department faculty,
submitted by Kitty Daniels*

Class: Any intermediate or advanced technique class

Objectives: To encourage students to reflect on their personal learning process, set personal goals, and take responsibility for their learning and growth; to facilitate communication between student and teacher, enabling them to develop mutual goals for students to focus on

Overview: Two letters written to the teacher: one early in the semester and one at the end

Dear Students:

As your teacher, I would like to get to know you better as dancers! Since we value self-reflection, self-assessment, and interior awareness in our students, it might be helpful both for you and for me if you write two informal letters addressed to me during the semester. Please type the letters so that I can read them easily. Here are the guidelines for each letter:

First Letter (Due at Beginning of Term)

You are a proficient, experienced dancer with a sophisticated knowledge of yourself and your working process. Given that, please do the following:

1. Describe your technical journey last semester: What were you working on? In what areas did you experience growth? Were there any frustrations?

2. Identify your priority for this semester—perhaps the technical goal that you think will facilitate your dancing on multiple levels.

3. How do you plan to work on this priority goal? What learning strategies will you employ?

4. How can I help you with this process?

Second Letter (Due Near End of Term)

Reflect on your initial goals and your work during this entire semester:

1. Reflect on your accomplishments this semester in relation to your initial goals. What growth did you experience? Did you modify your goals as the semester progressed? What were your frustrations? How could you address those frustrations productively?

2. What do you think you need to work on to continue your growth?

3. Given your personal learning style and process, what is the best way for you to work toward these goals?

4. Do you have summer study plans that will help you to progress in these areas?

Kitty Daniels, MA, teaches at Cornish College of the Arts in Seattle, Washington.
From W. Oliver, 2010, *Writing About Dance* (Champaign, IL: Human Kinetics).

Journal Prompts Reflecting on Dance, Cognition, Culture, and Identity

Mira-Lisa Katz

Class: Any beginning studio dance class; this exercise was originally designed for high school students in a summer dance intensive

Objectives: To encourage self-reflection about thinking and learning in dance; to support motivation over the long term

Overview: Prompts for responses to be written in a journal; responses may then be shared with the class or a small group in discussion

Educational research on *metacognition*—the act of reflecting on our own thinking and learning processes—has shown that time set aside for such mental processing is time well spent. In addition to supporting memory, reflective talk and writing significantly enhance learning outcomes by anchoring students' attention in the activities at hand and sharpen their interest in key parts of their own learning process. Time devoted to writing reflectively also supports students' motivation to learn over the long term because they are better able to track their own accomplishments, development, and progress as dancers, thinkers, and artists.

Students engaged in reflective writing during the Shawl-Anderson Teen Summer Dance Intensive in Berkeley, California.

Photo by Mira-Lisa Katz.

Journal Prompts

- On a personal level, what have you found most interesting so far about this class? Make a short list or write a paragraph about the highlights and be ready to share your ideas with the group.

- Come up with at least seven metaphors, similes, images, or ideas that you associate with dance. Write them down in your dance journal, and be ready to share and compare your list with two or three other dancers in small groups. When you compared your lists, what was most interesting about them?

- How does dance *make you feel*? How does it affect you *emotionally* and *psychologically* as well as *physically*? Spend a couple of minutes writing about why you like to dance and describe how dance shapes other parts of your life. Jot down specific examples if you can.

- Has dancing allowed you to develop any personal qualities, skills, or ways of thinking that you've been able to bring into other areas of your life? Can you offer an example or two?

- What, if anything, has dance helped you to understand about the person you would like to become in the future? How might dance help you achieve this?

- How is learning dance similar to or different from the learning you do in school or in other parts of your life? Please jot down some specific examples. Do you think dance is like writing? In what ways might it be similar to or different from writing? How is dance like, or not like, reading?

- Did you see a performance recently that you found inspiring? What about it excited or moved you?

Feel free to write in some questions you'd like to use as writing prompts:

_____

_____

Teacher's note: It is interesting to have students write about one or more of these prompts more than once. Teachers might consider having the dancers compare their own answers over time to observe changes in their thinking and experience. In other settings, dancers have found this reflective phase very satisfying for the reasons noted at the beginning of the exercise.

Mira-Lisa Katz, PhD, teaches at Sonoma State University in Rohnert Park, California, and the Shawl-Anderson Dance Center in Berkeley, California.
From W. Oliver, 2010, *Writing About Dance* (Champaign, IL: Human Kinetics).

Artistic Statement

Jane Baas

Class: Dance composition, choreography, or senior seminar

Objective: To enhance students' awareness of the unique nature of their own choreography in a broader artistic context

Overview: Students develop a one-page written statement about the nature of their creative work

Teacher's note: This exercise was developed as part of the assessment process for the department of dance at Western Michigan University. Each dance major is required to write this statement in his or her first dance composition class and then revise it for the final senior seminar.

What is an artistic statement?

An artistic statement is a concise document written by the artist that explains the nature of his or her artistic work.

When is an artistic statement used?

It is used for exhibition purposes, grant applications, teaching position applications, fellowships, and more. It can be used in several ways, including pointing the viewer to the concerns that the artist considers to be important in the work and helping publicists and critics write about the work.

Instructions

Prepare your artistic statement in paragraph form, not to exceed 250 words. Please address the following questions:

- Why do you dance? What is your passion for dance? What role does dance play in your life?
- How do you view your own work as an artist in the context of dance history and current developments in dance?
- What are your aspirations for bringing valuable and original contributions to the field of dance?

Suggestions for Creating an Artistic Statement

- Clarify the conceptual parameters of your work in your own mind before you begin to write the statement (if you are unsure of what your work is about, your readers will be, too.)
- Who is your audience?
- Avoid editorializing or overexplaining, such as telling readers what to think about the work, or providing detailed explanations of intent.

- Keep your statement concise and to the point; one page is enough.
- Avoid using jargon and terminology that might be understood only by trained dancers.

Other Hints

- Have a friend ask you questions about your work. Answer the questions, record the conversation, or take notes.
- Have someone who doesn't know your work ask you questions.
- Read the statements or writings of artists with whom you have an affinity.
- Write in the first person.
- Speak as honestly as you can. Edit out phrases that are not specific to the work.
- Make the reader want to look at and know more about your work.
- Your statement should be more than just a description of your process.
- Use quotations *only* when they are absolutely relevant to your work.
- Have a faculty member read your statement while looking at your work.

Jane Baas, MFA, teaches at the University of Western Michigan in Kalamazoo.
From W. Oliver, 2010, *Writing About Dance* (Champaign, IL: Human Kinetics).

Class Observation

Kitty Daniels

Class: Any studio dance class

Objectives: To provide a format for observations by students who are sitting out during class because of illness or injury; to help students develop self-reflection, critical analysis, and constructive criticism skills

Overview: Students write the answers to the following questions while observing class

Sometimes, students are not able to dance during class because of illness or injury. Since attendance is so important in dance class, students may be encouraged to stay and observe class in order to learn what they can. Answering questions about class while observing helps students stay focused and encourages critical thinking.

Kitty Daniels, MA, teaches at Cornish College of the Arts in Seattle, Washington.
From W. Oliver, 2010, *Writing About Dance* (Champaign, IL: Human Kinetics).

CLASS OBSERVATION FORM

Name _____ Class _____ Date _____

1. Why are you sitting out? If you are injured, are there ways that you could still participate in the class?

   _____

2. Mention three of the teacher's general or individual feedback comments. How does this feedback apply to you?

   _____

3. Do you see students responding to the teacher's feedback? Name specific students and explain what you see.

   _____

4. What positive interactions do you see between the teacher and the students? What allows the teacher to function successfully? What allows the students to function successfully?

   _____

5. How are students demonstrating commitment during this class?

   _____

6. Are there any students in the class who are inspiring to you? Why, specifically?

   _____

7. What do you notice about the relationship between the music and the movement? How are individual dancers responding to the music?

   _____

8. What images come to your mind while you watch the class? What do you see when you move to another area of the room?

   _____

9. How is observing this class a valuable part of your education?

   _____

10. How would you summarize what you've learned by observing this class?

    _____

From W. Oliver, 2010, *Writing About Dance* (Champaign, IL: Human Kinetics).

Quick Write

Wendy Oliver

Class: Any

Objective: To clarify thoughts before class discussion

Overview: Write for five minutes in response to a reading, video clip, or live movement

This simple exercise helps students organize their thoughts in preparation for a class discussion. It is a chance to reflect and make sense of a reading or viewing experience. It is easiest to do it in class immediately before discussion, but it could also be done at home ahead of time. The entire assignment, including the reading or viewing, can be done in class if the teacher selects either a very short article or a short dance as the focus for writing and discussion.

Assignment

Write for five minutes, nonstop, about your assigned reading, video, or other experience. Don't worry about organization, grammar, or spelling, because these responses will not be collected. Be prepared to share your observations and responses in discussion.

Sample Prompts for a Reading

- What did you learn?
- What are the most important ideas in this reading?
- What ideas did you especially agree or disagree with, and why?

Sample Prompts for Viewing of Video or Live Movement

- What did you observe about the movement?
- Were there any recurring movement ideas?
- What were the most outstanding features of the performance?

Teacher's note: If you've ever had a class that is shy about discussion, this exercise is very helpful. When students write down their thoughts, they become invested in them and more confident that they have something meaningful to contribute. As an alternative to a large-group discussion, students can share their thoughts in small groups in order to allow everyone more time to speak.

Wendy Oliver, MFA, EdD, teaches at Providence College in Rhode Island.
From W. Oliver, 2010, *Writing About Dance* (Champaign, IL: Human Kinetics).

Quick Write Variation for Technique Class

Wendy Oliver

Class: Technique class

Objective: To reflect on one's own dancing in class

Overview: Five minutes of writing at the end of class

Immediately after a dance class, you might feel great, frustrated, enlightened, or energized, to name a few possibilities. This is a chance to think about your technique and artistry as well as your struggles and accomplishments, for that class period.

Assignment

Write nonstop for five minutes on one or more of the following prompts:

- How am I feeling right now, and why?
- What did I learn today?
- What did I do well today?
- What did I find difficult today, and why?
- What can I do in the next class that will help with difficulties I had today?

Wendy Oliver, MFA, EdD, teaches at Providence College in Rhode Island.
From W. Oliver, 2010, *Writing About Dance* (Champaign, IL: Human Kinetics).

Creative Process Exercises

This group of exercises will stimulate your creativity and prompt self-awareness. All of these exercises ask you to step outside of your everyday self and take a new perspective on what you are doing. If you want to experience something new that could lead to interesting improvisation or choreography, try one of these!

Shower Assignment
Heidi Henderson

Class: Improvisation, dance composition, choreography

Objectives: To provide awareness of habitual movement; to explore alternatives in daily movement patterns

Overview: Students write a short, informal paper

I use this exercise in an improvisation class as part of weekly journal writing about the experiences of the work in class and how that work is reflecting or affecting self-knowledge and life outside of class.

This assignment provides insight into the power of habits in movement. Students, many of whom are shocked that they even have a habitual shower routine, learn how easily they are tied to habit, to routine. Other learning experiences include paying deeper attention at times when one is usually on autopilot, writing, and experiencing a movement idea that could be considered intimate from a neutral and objective viewpoint. Breaking a habit becomes a huge endeavor for some students.

Neuromuscular habit is a powerful force beyond your consciousness. Efficiency, expediency, and the pace of modern culture leave little room for daydreaming or for taking the time to wander through a change in daily movement patterns.

Assignment

Take a shower, but complete your shower tasks in a different order than you usually would. Write about your experience.

Writing Samples

These are writing samples from students in my improvisation class.

Student 1

It was a quiet morning in the town of New London. The people woke up, the nuclear submarines were getting their innards remodeled, everything was going according to plan. Then came the shower. There was something terrible about it, like some horrible slime crept on the person showering. The shower, my friends, was one out of sync; the showerer was your humble narrator.

So it happened upon much scrubbing, the feeling of dirtiness wouldn't go, wouldn't wash off. For you see the usual sequence of events in the shower was not followed. First, second, and third became third, first, and second. And if this amuses you, my friend, then all I have to say is that it did not amuse your humble narrator...

Then it occurred to me, my friends, it wasn't the shower that was so wrong, so to say, it was me. No rascal had switched the water for sweat; it was still good hot water that was pouring over my body. So logically it was me that created this ridiculous scenario in my head.

Student 2

I knew immediately once I picked up my shower container that this would be difficult. I had come prepared. Having decided the order of my new routine ahead of time, I had a false sense of security. This will be simple, I thought to myself as I approached the bathroom door. Momentarily it occurred to me that perhaps I should shower in a new stall. However, as quickly as that thought came to mind, I discarded it believing that this particular routine alteration might just be the end of me. I stepped into the shower and immediately hung my hair elastic on the lower door hook and my towel on the hook directly above it. I had already begun my usual routine. This would be far more difficult than I imagined. Once in the shower, I became frustrated and forgot the new routine that I had so skillfully made up. I had to wing it. I felt as if I had split personalities. I had to discipline and restrain myself from following the usual routine. After my shower, I did not feel clean. I thought about showering again but decided against it. I did not want to push my luck. I had already had a traumatic showering experience once; two in one day could lead to some crazy phobia.

Student 3

Truth be told, I generally take showers at a time when I am not particularly in the mood to challenge myself intellectually. On this particular morning, when I slipped on my shower flip-flops that were still moist from the morning before and squished my way out the door, bucket in hand, towel around my waist, I had two thoughts and only two thoughts going through my mind. They are as follows: 1. I really should replace my toothbrush, bristles almost horizontal. Maybe I can get my mom to send me a new one; parents are always willing to buy things like that for their children. 2. Oh, yeah, that journal assignment for dance class . . . take a shower in a different order.

No big deal, I thought. I'm not the kind of person who holds to patterns, except for a hot cup of coffee every morning . . . and then there is the way I always change my shirt first, then my pants. I drifted away from my actions, my thoughts digressed . . . and before I knew what I was doing, I was standing in the shower, valve turned three quarters to the left, nozzle emitting water at a familiar temperature, product bottles on the shower shelf, soap already in my right hand, moving in and out around my left armpit and shoulder (I start top left and finish bottom right). I was struck dumb, feeling like someone had just delivered some enlightening but tragic explanation of me. And in a way someone had delivered a defining headline . . . the reporter was me; there were no words because there did not need to be; and the news was that I *am* after all one of those people floating mindlessly through life. I have come to the conclusion that a sensitivity to action brings about emotional sensitivity—all this from a groggy shower?

Heidi Henderson, MFA, teaches at Connecticut College in New London.
From W. Oliver, 2010, *Writing About Dance* (Champaign, IL: Human Kinetics).

Using Poetry as a Structural Tool for Choreography

Christina Tsoules Soriano

Class: Dance composition

Objective: To develop knowledge of poetry and poetic structures as a creative springboard for choreography

Overview: Students use the structure of poems as the basis for potential dance ideas; students write their own poems with specific structures and use them as the basis for additional dances

I am drawn to working with poems as a pedagogical tool in a dance composition class because poems appear to be so beautifully vulnerable to me. Reading or reciting a poem, one has to honor every choice the poet makes in shaping that poem. I ask my beginning choreography students to read, write, and study many kinds of poems as a tool for generating movement. Particularly, my interest in poems as a pedagogical tool lies in a poem's physical structure. While I would not discourage students from composing a movement study based on or inspired by the content of a poem, I ask students to instead look at its skeleton or structural makeup on the page.

Examining Poems

Here are some potential questions to consider as you examine written poems:

1. Read the poem aloud and notice the rhythm associated with it. Is it even? Does the poem start and stop in natural places? How might movement choices you create reflect the rhythm of this poem?

2. Notice the poem's beginning and ending. What is its "entrance" and how can your movement studies mimic the energy or tempo of the poem's first line or words? Similarly, with the poem's ending, notice what it does. Does it apologize? Sound firm? Does it linger with an idea? How might your dance's ending follow these ideas?

3. Is there a clear rhyming structure in the poem? How can movement rhyme?

4. Is there a specific stanza structure? Perhaps there is one stanza with four lines, followed by another with three, and then another stanza that is five lines. Can your dance have "stanzas," or sections, that mimic this or other patterns?

5. Examine the length of a poem, line by line. Notice the clear intent that the poet has with each line, where one word ends a line and how it relates to the first word in the next line. Is there punctuation? Does it dangle as you read it aloud? How can you experiment physically with these ideas?

6. What spatial relationship does the poem have with the page? Is there a lot of blank, expansive space? Does the poem start at the top of the page? In the middle? How much space is between each section? What does this encourage you to think about in relation to time and spatial choices in your movement study?

Suggested Poems

The following poems are just a few I have consistently shared with my students and found to be successful examples. Certainly, there are thousands of beautiful poems that would be equally powerful, and I encourage teachers to rediscover their favorite poems as a pedagogical tool.

- "Do Not Go Gentle Into That Good Night" by Dylan Thomas
- "Departure" by Carolyn Forché
- "Grandmother's Song" by Nellie Wong
- "A Slumber Did My Spirit Seal" by William Wordsworth
- "Mindful" by Mary Oliver

Additional reading: *Nine Gates*, by Jane Hirschfield (1998)

Writing Poems

Students are also encouraged to write several kinds of poems. These student-written poems may also serve as the basis for dances.

1. The *haiku*, in its 5-7-5 structure, is a brilliant way to encourage students to push beyond movement generation in the familiar, tired, eight-count structure. By infusing movement with a 5-7-5 rhythmic quality, movement becomes more unpredictable and students realize that movement ideas do not have to stop at count 8.

> Wind whips from the north
> Leaves sweeping across the path
> Winter, is that you?

2. *Onomatopoeia* is a wonderful tool that allows students to tap into the sound of movement possibility. Examples of onomatopoeic words are *hiss, snap,* and *murmur*—words in which the formation or use of words imitates their representative sounds. If you try to imitate these words, innovative movement ideas inevitably result.

3. The *concrete* poem is much like *opta*matopoeia (my word creation). The concrete poem's visual reality expresses a poet's decision to place words on the page in a nonlinear formation that may be shaped or scattered. Using this type of visual representation on the page can translate to the student choreographers' exploration of multiple spatial possibilities in the studio.

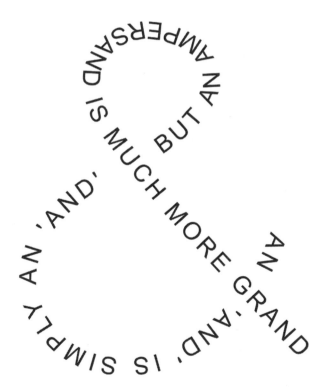

Ampersand. Concrete poem by Patrick Winstanley.

Courtesy of Patrick Winstanley

Christina Tsoules Soriano, MFA, teaches at Wake Forest University in Winston-Salem, North Carolina. From W. Oliver, 2010, *Writing About Dance* (Champaign, IL: Human Kinetics).

Intention Framing for Choreography

Larry Lavender

Class: Dance composition

Objective: To clarify students' artistic thinking and to increase their awareness of relationships between artistic ideas and emerging artistic forms

Overview: Informal writing on your choreographic intentions (including methods, motives, and goals) to be repeated occasionally during the creation of a work

Choreography is a complicated thing to do. For one thing, dances never stay put; when rehearsal ends the dance walks out the door with the dancers! And even when the dancers (and the dance) are present, there are so many artistic options available that the whole process can be scary. To sort things out and maintain a sense of flow, most choreographers do a great deal of thinking about their dances both during rehearsals and in periods between. They mull over various aspects of their short- and long-term plans, assess their work methods, reflect on the performance and presentation of the movement itself, and wonder constantly about how best to manage their dancers' talents and energies. It is amazing how many decisions choreographers make, and how often they have to make (and possibly unmake) decisions while creating a work.

Research on human problem solving in both scientific and artistic domains shows that people who think about their thinking—that is, who regularly review their plans, assumptions, expectations, and personal reactions to their work—have a smoother and more rewarding experience than people who remain more or less blind to their habits of thinking. Interestingly, the idea of thinking about your own thinking has a name: *metacognition*. If that sounds overly fancy, don't worry—learning to "do" metacognition is pretty easy.

As a choreographer, a good first step in learning how to think about your thinking is to freely jot down thoughts (or sentence fragments) about what you are trying to do and how you may go about it. Once you have even a few notions on paper (and you might find yourself scratching out a few before you find ones to keep), the next step is to crystallize your ideas into more concrete choreographic intentions. Try to set your ideas into one or more of the following choreographic intention frames:

> "I am making a dance by . . ." (write one or more *processes* for creating the work).

"I am making a dance in which . . ." (write *images* you imagine the work will contain).

"I am making a dance that . . ." (write *outcomes* you hope the work will achieve).

"I am making a dance about . . ." (write *themes or subject matter* for the work).

The following discussion will clarify the various kinds of intention frames:

•   **Process intentions** are often based on emotions: "I want to explore loneliness, so we'll improvise phrases based on feeling lonely, and I will create the dance from there." In contrast, design-based process intentions, such as the following from choreographer Lucinda Childs, are common: "I was interested in exploring what would happen when two dancers paced an eighteen-count phrase on a semicircular path while the other two dancers were executing a phrase of the same duration on a floor pattern that covered three quarters of a circle" (Morgenroth 2004, 75).

•   **Image intentions** clarify pictures of the dance that a choreographer has in mind. Here is an example: "I want to create a rough-and-tumble duet, a struggle, with a lot of angular, distorted movement."

•   **Outcome intentions** are imagined by choreographers who envision their dance will lead to, or cause, particular results. Choreographers who feel strongly about events in society and in the world often imagine laudable social or political outcomes. For example, a choreographer might say, "I want to motivate people to do something about . . ." (a particular issue or cause).

•   **Aboutness intentions** arise when choreographers have clear ideas about the subject matter of their work. An example is "I am making a dance about heartbreak" (or jealousy, or life under the sea).

In playing with this exercise, do not be surprised if more than one intention frame is attractive to you. **Patchwork intentions** may combine several of the other types of intention. For example, "I imagine smooth, gliding electronic music and randomly patterned group dancing sections (image intentions) that we create improvisationally (process intention). I feel this dance will be about layers of identity (aboutness intention), and I hope the audience members will learn a lot about themselves (outcome intention)."

Intention framing can be done as an in-class or out-of-class exercise. It can be exciting to do it regularly—the night before each rehearsal, for instance. Regular repetitions of the exercise will teach you a great deal about how your mind is processing the twists and turns of the dance-creation process and about the ways in which ideas can shift over time. Don't be surprised if the nature of your intentions changes a lot during the weeks you spend creating a work. This often happens as a dance evolves and begins to tell the choreographer more and more about what it wants to be. In any case, it is important to allow your ideas (and your dance) to evolve rather than to force things to stay just as they are at the beginning.

Larry Lavender, PhD, teaches at University of North Carolina at Greensboro.
From W. Oliver, 2010, *Writing About Dance* (Champaign, IL: Human Kinetics).

Focus on Writing Exercises

This group of exercises will help you improve your writing. One of the most difficult challenges in writing about dance is to describe it in a vibrant way. These exercises offer various ways to describe and analyze dance and can serve as preparation for writing a dance critique.

Dancing to Write, Writing to Dance

Rachel Straus

Class: Dance composition or any studio dance class

Objectives: To make connections among seeing, writing, and moving; to improve self-awareness, critical thinking, and descriptive writing

Overview: Two assignments that involve teaching and learning movement, watching movement, and writing about it

At some point in dance writers' careers, most feel compelled to experience the sweaty side of the art form. Alastair Macaulay, chief dance critic of the *New York Times*, described attempting petit allegro jumps in the privacy of his home. Joan Acocella, dance critic for the *New Yorker*, studied dance as a child. Wendy Perron, editor in chief of *Dance Magazine*, performed with the Trisha Brown Dance Company. As a writer for five dance publications, I love to dance. My class-taking experience recently reached the quarter-century mark. Studying dance keeps me connected on a gut level with the art form. It also informs and improves my critical writing. Like a dancer seeking full-bodied physicality and grace, I seek to describe with vivid words the energy, emotional arc, and visual qualities of a performance. In reviews I include at least one detailed description of what a dancer did with his or her body. Hopefully, that sentence gives the reader a visceral experience. Following are two exercises I've used to bridge the divide between dancing with my body and writing with my mind.

Assignment 1

Part A: Select a dance phrase you were taught that covers space, involves dynamic changes, and is at least 36 counts long. After class, rehearse the phrase several times until it becomes part of your muscle memory. Then teach it to a classmate whose movement quality you admire.

Part B: Several hours later or the next day, ask your classmate to dance the phrase. Write a paragraph about what you see with the aim of describing it to someone who has never seen the dance. Do any visual metaphors come to mind? Does the movement belong to a recognizable style? What is its mood? Is it virtuosic or pedestrian? What are its rhythmic qualities? Because you can feel the dance phrase in your body, notice if your language has more specificity, more active verbs, or immediacy. Hopefully it will. Now invert the exercise.

Assignment 2

Watch a dance phrase (no longer than one minute) that you are able to see at least twice. (It could be from a video, a class, or a rehearsal.) Write a paragraph about what you see. Use the previous questions, if needed, as a guide. Focus on what you find most compelling or mysterious or, if neither of these characteristics exists, why it lacks great interest. Then learn the phrase. While learning the movement, notice aspects of it that you missed when looking at it. Notice if there are any moments that are physically challenging but didn't look to be so. Notice the speed: Does it feel faster or slower than it looks? Does it incorporate more of the body than you were aware of? Does dancing it evoke an emotion such as melancholy, exuberance, or tranquility?

Conclusion

Compare your first experience of dancing and then writing with your second experience of writing and then dancing. Which of the two pieces of writing do you prefer? Which one used words that better capture the movement vocabulary? Which one was easier to write?

Rachel Straus, MA, is a Dance Magazine writer and PhD candidate at University of Roehampton, London, UK.

From W. Oliver, 2010, *Writing About Dance* (Champaign, IL: Human Kinetics).

Observation and Description Exercise

Stephanie L. Milling

Class: History, choreography, movement analysis, technique (any class requiring observational and descriptive skills)

Objective: To develop skills in movement observation and description (with minimal interpretation)

Overview: Descriptive exercise based on watching three online dance excerpts

I used this exercise in courses titled Dance, Gender, and Culture, and World Dance Forms. It is a catalyst for further analytical description and was originally developed because I needed a way to communicate clearly to my online students how to observe and describe movement with minimal interpretation. Of course we cannot remove how we see from the cultural values that underpin our seeing. However, I wanted the students to observe like anthropologists observe in the field, with an etic* perspective. I believe that we cannot properly analyze and interpret a dance without having an understanding of its cultural, historical, or social underpinnings. This exercise was the first in a string of assignments that prepared them for their performance interaction paper, which they turned in at the end of the semester.

------

* etic: involving analysis of cultural phenomena from the perspective of one who does not participate in the culture studied, as opposed to *emic*, where the person studying the culture also participates in it.

Assignment

View three of the following:

Swan Lake (video clip): www.houstonballet.org/Ticketing_Schedule/ Swan_Lake_Preview (Swan Lake pas de deux, Houston Ballet)

Balinese Legong Dance (video clip): www.youtube.com/ watch?v=f30egPFCm-g&feature=relate

Ghanaian Dance (video clip): www.alokli.com/site/video.vd/ of02bawa2.mpg

Contact Improvisation (video clip): www.youtube.com/ watch?v=NrIxZ9kG5VA (scenes from 2006 Body Research Contact Improv Gathering 3)

Note: Video clips change frequently, so those listed here may no longer be available; you may find alternatives by searching YouTube.

Write

In my experience, people have an easier time interpreting movement than describing it. To start your movement description, take a piece of paper and a pen. Draw a line down the middle of your paper. On one side write *what* and on the other side write *how*. As you watch the video clips, write down *what* the dancers do and *how* they do it. For example:

What	How
Jump	Jubilantly
Roll	Violently
Point	Angrily

Traditional Balinese dance performed in Bali, Indonesia. Use a video clip of a dance such as this one to help hone observation and description skills.

© Franck Iren/age fotostock

Use adjectives, adverbs, and verbs in your description. After you have made a list, write your description in a narrative form as if you were giving a vivid account of the performances to another person. The description of each clip should be at least five sentences in length with correct grammar, spelling, and punctuation and good organization. Please incorporate approaches suggested in the readings. Hand in a hard copy or post your description on your class online discussion board.

Your descriptions will be evaluated by their level of detail and thoroughness, which will indicate the level of your observation skills. The description should provide a reader who has not seen the performance with a visual image of it.

Teacher's note: Almost any videos could be used for this exercise. This exercise is especially helpful when asking students to watch dance forms they are not familiar with because it asks them to see what the dancers are doing without immediately placing judgment or cultural bias on what they see. The suggested readings assist students in understanding some ways of approaching movement description.

Suggested Readings

See references section in the back of the book for full citations.

"Sense, Meaning, and Perception in Three Dance Cultures" by Cynthia Jean Cohen Bull (1997)

"Beyond Description: Writing Beneath the Surface" by Deborah Jowitt (2001)

Stephanie L. Milling, PhD, teaches at Winthrop University in Rock Hill, South Carolina.
From W. Oliver, 2010, *Writing About Dance* (Champaign, IL: Human Kinetics).

Dance in a Ritual Context

Elizabeth Cooper

Class: Cross-cultural dance, dance history, dance and society, dance appreciation

Objectives: To recognize, reflect on, and be able to articulate essential components of dance movement; to understand that dance is a form of human expression as well as a means of communication; to understand how dance is a reflection of societal values and world views

Overview: In-class writing exercises based on video clips; out-of-class writing assignment based on creating and describing a dance ritual

I use this exercise in the course Cross-Cultural Dance, which looks at a variety of theatrical and nontheatrical dance forms and how they function in various societies. It asks students to write from a kinesthetic perspective (how the movement feels when performing it).

Teacher's note: We prepared for this work using in-class writing assignments based on video clips. Students practiced analyzing what they saw with regard to space, time, and dynamics and the relation between dancers (and musicians), then reflected on how context was connected to function and meaning. Students also compared two cultural dance forms in order to discern movement preferences and how the essential components of the dances could be understood as a reflection of societal values.

Assignment

Create a ritual in which dance is an integral and embedded component. Begin by describing your ritual. Include in this description the functions of the ritual, the setting (such as locale or time of day), and the number and roles of the participants (this may include spectators and participants from the ancestral or spirit world). What is the importance of your ritual to the community?

Brainstorming: Write down some common occasions for performing a ritual. Choose one of these or create something new. Close your eyes and envision this imagined ritual and its dance. Jot down what you see. Do your best to get inside the dancing body. Imagine that you are various participants playing different roles.

Next, develop your ideas more fully through the use of descriptive language, active sentences, analogy, and simile. Include in this section a discussion of what the dance *looks* like from the outside and *feels* like from the inside. Who is dancing and how does the dancer relate to other people present at the ritual? What is being communicated through the dance? Is music present? Are props or fetishes necessary for the ritual to be performed properly and successfully?

Finally, discuss the result of the ritual and its dance. Did the performance of the ritual transform the participants in any way? In other words, were they different at the conclusion of the ritual than at its commencement? How so?

Assess your work: Read what you have written aloud to yourself and to a peer. What does your narrative enable you to see, hear, feel, smell, and taste with regard to the ritual?

Extra credit: Re-create your ritual and dance with classmates and perform it for the class (get us to participate if you like) or make a video that we can watch together.

Elizabeth Cooper, MFA, teaches at the University of Washington in Seattle.
From W. Oliver, 2010, *Writing About Dance* (Champaign, IL: Human Kinetics).

Summary Paper

Doug Risner

Class: Dance appreciation, dance history, dance criticism, dance pedagogy, teaching methods, or any that require significant reading

Objectives: To develop students' reading and comprehension skills; to develop students' ability to articulate in succinct ways an author's primary arguments and rationale; to prepare students for informed and engaged in-class discussion of the assigned readings; and to prepare students for writing articulate and informed position papers during the second half of the semester

Overview: One two-page paper based on a reading

Assignment

You are expected to read all assigned daily readings and be prepared to discuss what you have read on the date it appears in the course outline schedule. To be prepared for the in-class discussion, you are required to write a two-page summary of the article or chapter assigned and bring it to class. (The paper must be typewritten in 12-point font, double-spaced, with standard margins.) Use all two pages as described.

The summary paper explains the focus of the article or chapter (what it is about) and gives a summary of the author's three or four major points and the author's rationale for such. Please note that a summary paper focuses only on a concise explanation of the author's main ideas and arguments (rationale). It is not an opinion, response, or position paper.

An effective summary paper includes these five characteristics:

1. Captures the author's primary ideas in a cogent and efficient manner
2. Articulates the theoretical and applied implications of the reading
3. Summarizes the author's arguments in a straightforward manner
4. Clarifies the author's rationale in concise ways
5. Highlights one important quote from the reading that distills the primary message of the reading

Here are students' examples from a unit in dance pedagogy focusing on social and cultural issues in education:

Sample: Ineffective Opening Paragraph

White Privilege: Unpacking the Invisible Knapsack, by Peggy McIntosh

This article gives a lot of examples of how being a white person gives you lots of privileges in school. Just because you're white and other students don't get these things. The article goes on to say that just because you're a white person you probably don't realize things like the color of Band-Aids are made for white people's skin. As future dance teachers, we need to look at these things and other things the article talks about that aren't fair to students who aren't white. Everyone can dance, but all of us need to think about these things to be good dance teachers. This article made me think that things like racism need to stop.

Instructor comments: Your paper shows that this reading was powerful for you as a future teacher and made you think about racism in a new way. Think more, though, about summarizing the article clearly in your first paragraph; also please reference the article appropriately. Save citing the examples you find powerful for later in your summary. Make sure you are writing in complete sentences (your second sentence is a fragment). Also, watch your use of "you're white"—who is *you* in "you're"? Many of your peers in this class are nonwhites, for example. In addition, watch your overuse of "things"—tell your readers clearly what these "things" entail. Last, think more about McIntosh's argument about "unearned privileges" and whiteness. What's the basis of her argument and what does it mean for teachers?

Sample: Effective Opening Paragraph

White Privilege: Unpacking the Invisible Knapsack

All too often, racism is understood as deliberately mean acts against a specific race or group of people. Peggy McIntosh[1] explains in her article "White Privilege" that racism is any imbalance of power between races, a result of either pushing one race down or raising one race above others. White privilege is the set of advantages that whites are granted by an unfair power structure, and that they are conditioned to be unaware of. McIntosh argues that as long as white privilege exists, so does racism, and that we must acknowledge its existence and decide how we plan to level the playing field. In order to create an environment of true equality and fairness, we need to eliminate the harmful privileges and make the positive ones "unearned entitlements" for all people (McIntosh, 242).

[1] McIntosh, Peggy. 2006. White privilege: Unpacking the invisible knapsack. In Shapiro, H., Latham, K., & Ross, S. (Eds.), *The Institution of Education.* 5th Ed. Boston: Pearson, pp. 238-242.

Instructor comments: Your growing strength in writing of summary papers contributes not only to your reading skills for clarity and application but also to your sensitive leadership example in our in-class discussions; thank you. Working from your strengths, let's work to hone your writing further: Watch your usage of "we." You probably want to clarify who "we" is, especially in this unit on social and cultural diversity—dance educators? future teachers?

Doug Risner, PhD, teaches at Wayne State University in Detroit, Michigan.
From W. Oliver, 2010, *Writing About Dance* (Champaign, IL: Human Kinetics).

Wrap-Up

Informal writing exercises can help you become more aware of yourself and of others, boost your creativity, help you set creative and technical goals, and improve your observation and writing skills. All of these things are helpful not only within the context of your dance classes but also in other classes and settings. Some of the *focus on writing* exercises at the end of this chapter are excellent preparation for writing a dance critique—perhaps the most common dance paper assignment at universities throughout the United States. Critiques are discussed at length in chapter 4.

Dance Critiques

Have you ever had an assignment in which you had to review a live dance concert? Did you wonder what was important for you to observe and how to respond in writing? This is the tricky task of dance criticism.

Dance criticism is writing that describes and discusses a dance performance in an illuminating way. Professional critics for newspapers and magazines often write about current performances in order to describe and evaluate them for potential ticket buyers. They also write to educate the public about what is happening in dance, pointing out interesting choreographers or dance companies. Critics who publish in magazines or academic journals have a longer time line and may write about several different performances in one article. The focus of their work may be to explore and analyze a particular choreographer, company, or style. Professional critics have a passion for dance writing that enables them to share their insights with others.

Dance reviews, response papers, and critiques are all similar to each other, but each has a unique connotation. Reviews are generally written by professionals for newspapers or magazines, and they rely on the critic's extensive background knowledge—knowledge that students don't yet have. Response papers are written by students, but the term suggests that the writer's emotional response is the most important element of the paper. The word *critique* suggests a thoughtful discussion and analysis and is the best term for a student assignment.

Students write dance criticism because teachers ask them to, but there are sound reasons for giving these assignments. Writing about a performance helps clarify your observations and responses to it and calls for both creative and critical thinking. You must be creative to find and use evocative words in your descriptions, and you are creative as you make inferences about possible meanings for a piece. You use critical thinking when you analyze various aspects of a dance and when you support your responses with concrete observations. You also use critical thinking when you choose which information to use, how to shape it, and what points need to be made about it.

As you write, you develop your aesthetic taste, or judgment, about what makes a work good. The more work you see and write about, the more sophisticated your judgments become. Writing is an essential part of learning to appreciate dance; it is a way of understanding dance more deeply and fully than is possible by simply observing it.

Watching and writing about live performances like this one by Australia's Tap Dogs develops your aesthetic taste. Sheldon Perry and Mitchell Hicks perform on a moving steel structure in Sydney, Australia.
© ROB ELLIOTT/AFP/Getty Images

Feldman Model of Criticism

Before you can critique a dance, you must observe it. The process of observation is not necessarily orderly; as you watch the colors, shapes, and movement of a dance, you are mixing the processes of perceiving, thinking, and feeling and are unlikely to have a coherent, all-encompassing statement to make at the moment the dance ends. Art educator Edmund Feldman recognized this problem:

> [T]here is a systematic way of acting like a critic, just as there is a systematic way of behaving like a lawyer. For lawyers there is a form for presenting evidence, refuting adversaries, citing precedents, appealing to jurors, and so on. Although art criticism does not have the form of legal debate, it *does* have form. To do criticism well, consistently, we need a form or system that makes the best use of our knowledge and intelligence and powers of observation. (1987, 471)

Feldman proposed to his visual arts students that criticism include description, analysis, interpretation, and evaluation, which are equally applicable to observing and writing about dance. He suggested that each step is necessary to the ones that follow, and for that reason, they should be undertaken in order. This means that thorough and accurate description is the basis for all other aspects of criticism; judgment and opinion need to be withheld until the end of the process.

Description is a straightforward recounting of what you see and hear. It is focused on the individual elements of a dance rather than on the whole. Analysis, on the other hand, explains how the parts fit together to make the whole. Interpretation involves a personal reading of either the entire work or aspects of it; this is where the critic's imagination is fully involved in finding meaning in the work. Evaluation is your considered judgment of the work, which may be either implicitly or explicitly stated. Using Feldman's model of criticism as modified for dance in figure 4.1, you can examine any dance work in detail and begin to make sense of it.

Writing a dance critique is a process that challenges you to describe, analyze, interpret, and evaluate dance in a compelling way. Obviously, you can't begin to write a critique until you have seen the performance that you will review, but what else is important

Model for dance criticism

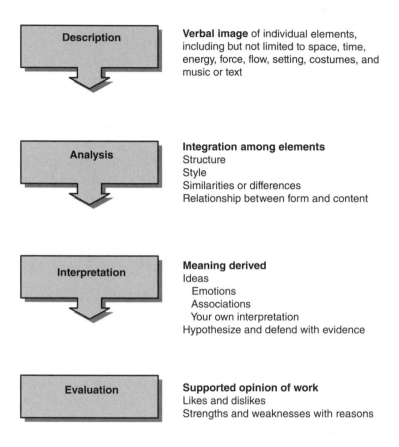

Description — **Verbal image** of individual elements, including but not limited to space, time, energy, force, flow, setting, costumes, and music or text

Analysis — **Integration among elements**
Structure
Style
Similarities or differences
Relationship between form and content

Interpretation — **Meaning derived**
Ideas
   Emotions
   Associations
   Your own interpretation
Hypothesize and defend with evidence

Evaluation — **Supported opinion of work**
Likes and dislikes
Strengths and weaknesses with reasons

Figure 4.1   The Feldman model.
Adapted from E. Feldman. 1987, *Varieties of visual experience* (New York: Harry N. Abrams).

to know and do before and during the writing process? The rest of this chapter answers that question. Although each element of the process is presented separately here, writing is actually more holistic and intuitive than following a to-do list. As described in chapter 1, writing is a circular process that involves writing itself, reviewing your writing, contemplating your writing, and making changes, so keep this in mind as you work.

Preparation

Your teacher has assigned a dance critique of a live performance and you are planning to see the American Indian Dance Theater when they come to town this weekend. What can you do to prepare? You could read about the company on their Web site and read articles in the paper, magazines, or books. Your dance program may have DVDs that you could watch and discuss with classmates, or there may be a digital video available online. When you understand something about a company's style, it makes it easier to describe and analyze the performance. It is especially helpful to do some reading about dance styles or genres that are unfamiliar to you. In addition to reading up on particular dance styles, you can read about specific choreographers who are involved in the show you will see.

Many shows are choreographed by one or more well-known choreographers, such as Twyla Tharp's *Movin' Out* on Broadway, or the New York City Ballet's *Nutcracker* by George Balanchine. In this case, it is easy to look up the choreographers online or in the library and get some in-depth information. Even when the choreographers are not nationally known, they may have a Web page or local press coverage. When you arrive at the show, before the performance begins, read the program carefully for notes about the choreographers, company, and dances.

Observation and Note Taking

Intelligent observation is a skill that can be acquired through attention to specific aspects of performance. Professional critics suggest that in observing, you should start with a "clean slate," trying to analyze as little as possible while the performance is in progress. While the acts of perception and analysis cannot be totally separated, premature analysis and judgment can distract from the sensory experience of observation. Critic David Vaughn says the following:

> You try to keep your visual imagination open while you are watching and not let any conscious thinking interfere with the process of receiving all these stimuli . . . the moment you begin thinking and forming sentences in your mind, you're cutting yourself off from the actual, immediate experience of watching. (Meltzer 1979, 15)

A critic's engagement with a performance begins with perception of the dancers executing the choreography. Thus, the two most basic aspects of the performance are the dancers and the movement itself. The supporting elements (music, costumes, lighting) are also important and must be viewed as part of the total experience. Look at the dance as a whole; let yourself be open to the various sights and sounds as you perceive them without trying to interpret them on the spot. However, do take some detailed notes of outstanding moments in the piece. This detail will be the basis for vivid description as you write your paper.

Once the show is over, you will move from experiencing the performance to a kind of "fermentation" process where thoughts are brewing, either consciously or unconsciously. This is a good time to discuss your initial responses with others in the audience, because it will help you begin to articulate your reactions. From here, you are ready to begin writing.

During the performance, note taking is strongly advised—it is difficult to remember much detail without some notes. Take a notebook with you so you can jot down observations during the performance. (You may want to practice writing in the dark.) Professional critic Marcia Siegel (1976, 28) says, "If I'm going to write about it, I take notes while it's going on. I'll write down really specific things that will help me to remember the facts about the events." Accurate description calls for attention to detail. Critic Deborah Jowitt says, "Either somebody's hands were crossed or they weren't crossed. In the case of dance, people make the most incredible mistakes both in fact and interpretation" (Meltzer 1979, 15).

The difficulties of note taking during a performance are the darkness and the distraction. The darkness of most theatrical performances makes it nearly impossible to see what you write. Also, looking at a notebook (or attempting to) detracts your eyes from the stage, causing you to lose some of the movement. Solutions to these problems include learning to take notes in the dark without looking at the page and taking notes between dances rather than during them. During intermission or after the performance, you may extend your notes, filling in what was hastily jotted down. (See Tips for Taking Notes at a Performance in chapter 2, p. 14, for further suggestions.)

The program serves as a crucial reference point and guide. Some viewers like to write directly on their programs. However, there is rarely enough space on a program for adequate notes, so it is best to bring a notebook. The program and whatever notes were taken will be your only concrete connection to the performance during the writing process, so it is important to record at least some of the event and impressions it created. Take notes of specific details, including how the dance begins and ends, how it is structured, how many dancers are in it, color and type of costumes, lighting, type of music, and general movement style. It's impossible to record all the movement you see, so select a few specific things from each dance or section, and note the general movement quality of each. To save time, use descriptive words and phrases rather than complete sentences.

Getting Started: Free Writing

As mentioned in chapter 2, free writing refers to writing without planning or self-judgment, usually for 10 to 20 minutes. Before beginning to free-write, ask yourself this question: "What stood out in the performance, and why?" Let yourself write uninterrupted, without worrying about grammar, punctuation, or coherence. The main goal is to let your thoughts and impressions bubble to the surface, where you can capture them on the page in front of you.

Many professional critics describe a moment where some image from the performance made a lasting impression. David Vaughn said the following:

> There may be some particularly arresting dance image that you want to keep in your head, because it seems to encapsulate the whole piece, or it's such a vivid image that you think if you describe it, you will give a better sense of what the dance was like rather than an overall description. (Meltzer 1979, 32)

You may also experience a "flash" like this. If you have a striking image to work with, write about that. If not, start with any idea from the performance that seems important or interesting to you. Many times, even if you do not begin with a strong mental picture of a dance, kinetic images will come back to you as you begin writing.

Once you have finished your free-writing exercise, go back and read what you've written. Within this loosely written mixture of thoughts and images, you will find material for your critique. Often, the direction for your entire paper may be gleaned from this exercise.

The next step is to take selected ideas and images from your free writing and use them as the basis for a more formal piece of writing.

As noted in chapter 2, the audience you are writing for is your peers. Keep this in mind as you decide how much and what kind of information to include in your paper.

Overview Approach

Professional critics have little need for guidelines with regard to style and organization; in fact, many writers have created their own successful approaches that are quite different from the basic one suggested here. Until you have developed considerable experience with critiquing, however, you will find it useful to learn the following overview approach to critiquing dance. This approach combines aspects of professional newspaper criticism with that of traditional essays.

An overview critique gives the reader an impression of the entire dance performance through both specific detail and general observations. A person who has not attended the performance should be able to read your overview and feel well informed about the event. Because it is impossible to discuss every aspect of a performance in three to four pages, you need to select the kind and amount of material to be included—that is, generally whatever you found most provocative or compelling. There is no need to try to find common ideas among the dances in a concert; instead, you should focus on what is unique or interesting about each one.

This type of critique is especially appropriate for the typical college or high school dance concert that includes many unrelated pieces. It can also be excellent for a professional company's work where more than one dance is presented, because it gives you a chance to explore each piece on its own individual merits. In addition to discussing individual works in some detail, a critique always gives some mention of the concert as a whole.

Construction

A critique needs an introduction, a body, and a conclusion. The introduction, usually one paragraph, lets the audience know what you are writing about, including the date and place of the performance, the name of the dance company, and other general information. It also catches the reader's attention with an interesting remark or observation about the experience.

The body is the substance of your paper; it holds your main thoughts about the experience and includes one or two paragraphs about each dance that you have chosen to discuss. The concluding paragraph is your summary, your final observations, and a way of giving closure to your critique. Your conclusion draws together your thoughts on the works that stood out and on the concert as a whole.

Suggested Format for Critique

This structure is a good way of organizing your critique, but it is not the only way. For instance, some writers like to begin immediately with movement description and work in the "who, what, when, where" information later in the paper. However, this particular format is good for beginning dance writers because it prompts a systematic consideration of three or four dances as well as the concert as a whole.

I. Introduction

   A. General information about the performance (who, what, when, where)

   B. Interesting assertion (thesis) about the performance as a whole

II. Body

   A. Dance 1, thesis sentence (analytical, interpretative, or evaluative)

      1. Performance detail

      2. Performance detail

      3. Performance detail

   B. Dance 2, thesis sentence

      1. Performance detail

      2. Performance detail

      3. Performance detail

   C. Dance 3, thesis sentence

      1. Performance detail

      2. Performance detail

      3. Performance detail

III. Conclusion
   A. Summary of points
   B. Response to concert as a whole
   C. New insight

Content

Because of limitations of space, the three- to four-page critique focuses on the most compelling aspects of the performance. The first task is to select the kind and amount of material that you would like to include. If you attend a performance that includes three or fewer dances, it should be possible to discuss them all in the space provided. Should the show consist of one full-length work, find three or four specific dance sections to critique. If the performance includes a large number of shorter dances, choose three or four of them to discuss. The way to make this selection is to ask yourself which of the dances are most provocative or evocative for you—these won't necessarily be the dances that you like the best, although that is a strong possibility.

For each of the dances that you have selected to discuss, you will need to find and highlight its outstanding features. It is impossible (and boring for the reader) to detail every aspect of any dance; the trick is to be complete without a blow-by-blow description. Be sure to include the names of choreographers, composers, and soloists where appropriate.

Thesis Sentence for Paper

The thesis for your critique should appear near the beginning of your paper, most likely in your introduction, and should comment on the concert as a whole rather than focus on one dance. Whether you have seen a performance with many works by different choreographers or a single, evening-length work, you will need to write a thesis that offers an interesting insight and refers to the concert as a whole. For a concert in which the work was all by one choreographer, this observation might be something about the choreographer's style. For a concert by diverse choreographers, your thesis will be more general. A dance critique does not need to prove a point in the same way a persuasive essay does.

Here are some examples of thesis sentences:

- In attending a dance concert at one of the nation's most diverse academic institutions, I certainly expected several dance styles to be showcased. However, my expectations for variety in the fall dance concert at Brown University were far surpassed.
- Each dance in *Riverdance* was so unique and distinct, and yet the show flowed perfectly and presented the audience with a very pleasurable experience.
- Two choreographers shared this show. Props played an integral role in the meaning and the impact of the pieces of both choreographers.

Thesis Sentence for Each Dance

In addition to your overall thesis, the discussion of each dance within the concert should include a thesis statement, which is like a topic sentence but is analytical, interpretive, or evaluative. Generally speaking, this statement will come at the beginning of the paragraph dealing with the dance in question, and the remainder of that paragraph will relate to that thesis sentence. This will help you to avoid making a list of unrelated facts that do little to convey a sense of the dance as a whole. You may use more than one paragraph to discuss a dance, but keep all writing on a specific dance connected to your thesis sentence for that dance. The thesis sentence for each dance that you discuss should be based on outstanding features of that dance and will necessarily be different for each of the dances in your overview. Once you have found something significant to say about each dance, you will use some combination of description, analysis, interpretation, and evaluation to illustrate your point.

Here are two examples of poor thesis sentences for individual dances; neither of them gives any analytic, interpretive, or evaluative information:

- "Yoked" was a quartet choreographed by Karen Swiatocha.
- The second piece, named "Serendipity," begins with three girls in the middle of the stage.

Here are some examples of good thesis sentences for individual dances:

- In "Dream State," choreographer Susan Smith examines the subconscious.
- Another dance that had many humorous qualities was "Going Places."
- If Taylor's audience had forgotten his wonderful ability to incorporate wit and satire in his choreography, their memory was certainly refreshed when the company performed his latest work.
- "Trio" was performed using large pieces of cloth to create interesting shapes that seemed to have a life of their own.
- "Between Us" was exuberant, fast-paced, and technically demanding.
- One dance did not seem to fit in with the rest of the concert.

Description, Analysis, Interpretation, and Evaluation

You've selected the dances that you want to write about, and you've come up with some interesting ideas about each of them. What's next?

Description, analysis, interpretation, and evaluation are at the heart of your paper, and each is important in conveying your thoughts to the reader. When you write, it's not possible or desirable to separate each of these modes of criticism—for instance, writing two paragraphs of description, two of analysis, and so forth. Instead, writing a critique requires a blending of the four modes with the goal of bringing the event to life for the reader. However, for the purposes of clarity, let's look at each mode separately.

Description

Description is used to give the reader a picture of the performance and is also crucial as the groundwork for analysis, interpretation, and evaluation. Someone who did not see the show should be able to read your paper and get a good idea of what the dance looked like. You should include both minute detail and broad overview in your writing. Take note of highlights or special moments in the dancing, and re-create them for the reader. These specific movement moments also provide a very particular kind of information that may be used to support interpretations and evaluations.

More generalized description of a dance or section of a dance is appropriate for capturing its flavor. Describing dance in great detail throughout the entire critique is neither possible nor appropriate. Instead, in attempting to summarize, you will be challenged to find ways of being comprehensive without being vague. Since you are writing an overview paper, remember also to give a descriptive impression of the concert as a whole.

Because dance is a language of movement and writing is a language of written symbols, there is a problem of translation between the two. Capturing on paper what you saw embodied onstage can be difficult. However, it is possible to capture the essence of that experience, and the following are some suggestions toward that end:

1. Use strong and varied action verbs, such as *slice, slither, melt,* and *propel*.

2. Use interesting adjectives, such as *tangled* arms, *piercing* leaps, *floating* turns.

3. Use colorful adverbs, such as leaned *heavily*, spiraled *briskly*, tumbled *fluidly*.

4. Avoid overuse of tired adjectives, such as *nice, good, bad, wonderful*.

5. Avoid hyperbole, such as *the worst, the best, the most*.

6. Use active rather than passive voice.

   • Active: The dancer gestured to her partner as the music changed tempo.

   • Passive: As the music changed tempo, the dancer could be seen gesturing to her partner.

Examples of Description in Professional Reviews

1. Here is a lively description of Miguel Gutierrez's *Everyone* excerpted from a review by Eva Yaa Asantewaa (2008, 82-83).

   > These dancers change like weather over open plains. Severe in one moment, they're smiling in the next, breaking loose in a wild, adolescent romp. . . . Then they settle into orderly exuberance, stomping in unison, a rhythm we feel in our own

feet on the resounding floor. Suddenly, as if cooling down after vigorous exercise, they flawlessly
execute a circular court dance of arcane, clockwork
complexity.

The author's evocative sentences use similes (*change like weather, as
if cooling down*) and vivid adjectives (*wild, adolescent, clockwork* complexity) to give the feeling of the dance.

2. Here is a specific description, or movement moment, from a
   review by Deborah Jowitt, writing in the *Village Voice* about the
   New York City Ballet's performance of George Balanchine's
   "Concerto, Opus 24" (1986, 99):

   > A man (Bart Cook) manipulates his partner
   > (Heather Watts) with gentle inquisitiveness.
   > Crouching down, he pushes her leg; she bends
   > it. . . he turns and lifts her while she's holding hands
   > in a circle of four women. Whatever he does with
   > her causes the wreath that she's part of to dip and
   > rise, close and expand.

This is excellent because it describes a point in the dance where Cook
and Watts have an interactive relationship. It shows how Cook's
actions cause a specific reaction in both his partner and the group
of women to which she is attached.

3. This example is a general descriptive opening followed by a
   movement moment. It is an excerpt from a review of Elizabeth
   Streb's company by Burt Supree (1991, 103) in the *Village
   Voice*:

   > In "Wall,". . .[the dancers] hurl themselves loudly
   > against a backboard at various angles—straight up,
   > sideways, flat—and drop and scramble away before
   > the next body hits. Or they hang there, piling one
   > on another. Two hang from the top edge, a third
   > twists and is caught on their bent calves. Some-
   > body is bundled up to the top, and the others get
   > underneath, upside down, and try to support him
   > as he slides slowly down. They plop belly-to-back
   > into a people sandwich.

This descriptive passage is full of wonderful action verbs: *hurl, drop, scramble, piling, bundled,* and *plop* as well as the image of "belly-to-back into a people sandwich." Supree manages to pack a lot of action into this short paragraph, giving readers the flavor of the movement, which is dynamic and varied.

Remembering and vividly describing a movement moment are perhaps the most difficult aspects of dance criticism. You can practice this skill by watching dance live or on videotape and writing about it, as in the writing exercises by Straus and Milling in chapter 3. You may also jot down your impressions of classmates during dance composition class or any other dance class where you have the opportunity to watch. All dance critiques need both movement moments and general description. Work to develop your writing skills so that your words evoke dance images for the reader.

Analysis

Analysis should focus mainly on what is seen within the framework of a single performance. However, if you have a broad dance background, you may certainly use that knowledge, when appropriate, in your paper. For instance, if you know something about the choreographic history of the artist whom you are critiquing, it may factor into your analysis of the movement or style. How the work is structured and how all the descriptive elements fit together form the basis of analysis.

To analyze the style of a dance, you need a passing familiarity with the movement vocabulary of ballet, modern, jazz, hip-hop, and other dance genres. The more dance you see, the more distinctions you will be able to make among these genres and their subcategories. For instance, African jazz and Broadway jazz are both types of jazz dance, but there are many differences between them. Often, there will be an overlapping of genres, and that, too, is important to note. Out of this composite picture comes an idea of the style of a particular work or choreographer.

Your analysis should include a discussion of how the dance fits together as a whole as well as its style. It might also include comparisons between sections of a dance or between two or more dances on the same program. Analysis assumes more knowledge than description. To analyze, a critic must be able to make comparisons, determine structures, or place things in context.

Examples of Analysis in Professional Reviews

1. Here, Deborah Jowitt (2008, 1) writes about a performance of Jerome Robbins' "The Goldberg Variations."

> Dancers play around in formal and not-so-formal ways and the choreographer sets himself exercises in canon and counterpoint (how many formations can he devise with two sextets? How many ideas can a canon convey about deconstructed unison?).

The analysis here is in the discussion of the structure that the choreographer uses. Jowitt has observed how Robbins has applied Bach's musical devices of canon and counterpoint to movement.

2. Here, Jack Anderson (1991, E3) analyzes choreography in a performance of a company from Sumatra, Indonesia:

> Martial arts were blended with dancing in the presentations of Gumarang Sakti Minangkabau, choreographed by Gusmiati Suid, the company's artistic director, and her son Boy GS. The choreography emphasized crouches and stances with bent knees that made the participants appear poised for battle.

Anderson uses his knowledge of martial arts to theorize that the choreographer used it as part of her vocabulary; he supports this assertion in the second sentence with his description and interpretation of the movement.

3. Claudia La Rocco (2008, E5) writes about a performance by Douglas Dunn & Dancers outdoors in lower Manhattan. This excerpt from the middle of the review uses the author's knowledge of historical dance to make a point about Dunn's style:

> Before founding [his company] he danced for master formalists (Merce Cunningham) and with master improvisers and game players (the Grand Union Collective), and his own style lies in both worlds.

Interpretation

Philosopher F.S.C. Northrop, in his book *The Meeting of East and West* (1946), divides visual art into two main categories. The first, which he calls "art in the first function" (407), is based on the idea that the medium is the message—in other words, the materials of art (or the medium): colors, shape, sound, and movement are arranged in a pleasing or interesting way. The aesthetic interest or pleasure derived from this arrangement is the focus of the work. The equivalent in dance is a choreographer who values movements, form, and design in an abstract way. For instance, modern dance choreographer Merce Cunningham believed that movement is intrinsically interesting and expressive and needs no narrative or theme to tie it together. However, no matter how abstract it may be, any dance is about something. A dance that takes movement as its subject may be about a particular kind of movement, such as weighted movement or spinning. Or it may focus on geometric design, partnering, or contrasts. Each of these elements may be considered subject matter for a dance.

On the other hand, Northrop (1946, 407) says, "Art in the second function . . . uses the aesthetic materials and the aesthetic continuum not primarily for their own sake, but . . . to convey some theoretically conceived factor in the nature of things, of which the aesthetic materials alone are the mere correlates or signs." In dance, that may be interpreted as work designed to convey a message or story. Here, the materials of the art become secondary to the message of the choreographer. In this case, the medium conveys the message. In dance, a story ballet such as *Swan Lake* and a Martha Graham work such as *Clytemnestra* are examples of dance as art in the second function.

Art can also fall between these two categories: art that is neither strictly abstract nor clearly a narrative. In a lecture addressed to a novice dance audience, choreographer Erick Hawkins (1967, 42, 44) describes a dance falling into this middle category: "In *Geography of Noon*, the dancers are four butterflies. But they in no way tell you any information about real butterflies. The dance just uses the metaphor of the butterfly, and then makes beautiful movement with it."

Context

All dances are made within a particular sociocultural context and relate to the traditions and values of that time and place. Knowing and understanding the varied kinds of human movement and expression that are typical of the cultural group making a particular dance are important in interpreting it. The movements of the dance have significance independent of the dance itself (Adshead 1988) and can be considered a kind of cultural knowledge (Sklar 2001). This applies to dance as a performing art as well as the many other functions of dance, including entertainment, religion, therapy, and socialization.

Because we are concerned here with dance as an art form, note that different views of what constitutes a dance coexist within the same country or region. The sociocultural diversity in the United States is expressed through the many accepted ways of making dances. Thus, there are expectations and values for each kind of dance that people may or may not be familiar with (Adshead 1988).

Problems in Interpretation

The meaning of a work, particularly in an unfamiliar genre, may not be immediately obvious, perhaps because dance is a more abstract art form than theater or film. Dance does not usually tell you in words what is happening onstage and how the dancers feel about it. However, that is one of the pleasures of interpreting dance—there is rarely only one correct interpretation of a work. Sometimes, the meaning of a piece is quite clear; at other times, you may discern two or more possible meanings; still other times, you may have no idea what to make of a dance. The best thing you can do is to make a case for your interpretation based on your observations and analysis. If you are confused, discuss why the piece was unclear.

Questions to Consider

After viewing the performance, you may find it useful to consider these questions as you think about your interpretation of what you saw. An answer to one of these questions might serve as the thesis sentence for your discussion of a particular dance, or it might provide an idea that you could use to frame the entire performance.

- **Title:** Does the title give any insight into the meaning of the dance? If so, how?

- **Program:** Does anything in the printed program give insight into the dance, such as names of characters in theatrical dances, explanations, text or poetry, or choreographer's notes?
- **Content:** Did this dance have a narrative, message, mood, or theme that you could identify? If it's abstract, what movement ideas and themes held it together? Is this dance art in the first or second function, or in between?
- **Cultural context:** Are you familiar with the cultural context in which the dance was created? If so, how might that help you interpret the work?
- **Personal meaning:** Were there any connections between what you saw in the performance and your own life experience? Were there specific movements that reminded you of something?

Interpretation involves forming a plausible hypothesis about the meaning of a dance and then backing it up. Examining the meaning of a piece (including work like Merce Cunningham's, which is quite abstract) is an important part of orienting yourself to it. If you are perplexed by a piece—perhaps you cannot tell whether it was intended to be abstract—it can be very interesting to explore why the dance was confusing to you. Sometimes, as an audience member, you may get the feeling that the choreographer was trying to convey something in particular, but you just didn't "get it." What is it in the dance that makes you feel this way? Is this a failing on your part, or was it a failing on the choreographer's part?

Any interpretation must be supported by evidence based on description, analysis, or knowledge presented in the program. For instance, if you believe that a modern dance choreographer was trying to make a point about competition in the business world, you must substantiate your claim with evidence. This evidence could be the nature of the movement, costumes, music, structure of the piece, or its title. When viewing dances of a country or culture you are unfamiliar with, program notes are obviously very useful; but if they are not available, the same principles apply: Support your interpretation with description and analysis. Interpretations and the reasons behind them often make good starting points for discussion about a dance.

Examples of Interpretation in Professional Reviews

1. Sometimes, an interpretation can be expressed as a metaphor, as it is here in Wendy Perron's (2008, 80) review of the Festival Ballet Providence:

> Viktor Plonikov's *Coma* (2007) begins with a stunning image of four dancers lying on slabs that are swinging close to the ground. It's a hospital with a difference. Banks of lights suddenly glare at us and go dark. Music by Arvo Pärt is played on tape (rather too loudly). In this context, the dancing seems to play out fantasies about death.

Perron has drawn on description to support her interpretation of the setting as a hospital and of the dance as a death fantasy. She has also included two elements that are evaluative: her use of the adjective *stunning* and her inserted remark about the music being too loud.

2. In the following example, Deborah Jowitt (1991, 75) explores the meaning of Christopher D'Amboise's dance "Runaway Train."

> Nothing in the neat choreography suggests anything runaway, and the two crossing paths of light laid on the floor . . . suggest an airport more than a railroad crossing. Or maybe that impression is created by the occasional semaphoring, some rather foolish blinking hand gestures, and the fact that the last image we see is LeBlanc aloft, arms spread, gleaming above a dark stage.

Jowitt relies on description to make her point: She notes that the light on the floor, the semaphoring, blinking hand gestures, and a dancer in a flying position all suggest to her the idea of an airport. The addition of the adjective *foolish* is an evaluative term that shows her negative take on this particular set of gestures.

Interpretation is an aspect of criticism in which the writer's imagination and creativity may be fully engaged. By allowing images from the dance to make visual or visceral impressions, you connect to your own subconscious dream world, where new ideas and feelings make their way into your consciousness as you write.

Evaluation

We all have opinions or subjective feelings about the dances we see. However, evaluation, or judgment of a dance, is not the same as expressing feelings about it. Evaluation builds on description, analysis, and interpretation to make arguments that show the strengths and weaknesses of a piece. Each dance genre has its own standards by which it is commonly judged; however, each dance in a genre is individual and no one list of standards will adequately cover every aspect of a dance that might be evaluated.

Additionally, the standards by which dances are judged are continually evolving. Rather than refer to a predetermined set of criteria, state what you believe to be the merits of the dance and then support your claim with reasons that are related to observable qualities of the dance. For further discussion , see *Dancers Talking Dance: Critical Evaluation in the Choreography Class* by Larry Lavender, pp. 32-37.

Note that liking a dance is not the same as judging it "successful." And disliking a work does not necessarily mean that it was unsuccessful. For instance, you might dislike a gloomy, depressing dance about war, but it may be successful because it manages to convey some of the qualities of war in a compelling way. These distinctions can be part of a discussion in your paper. It is appropriate to give your opinion of a dance, but be sure to let the reader know why you liked or disliked a particular dance. Point out what caught your attention during the performance, whether good or bad. Which elements compelled you to write about them, and why?

Examples of Evaluation in Professional Reviews

1. Sometimes, evaluative comments are directed toward particular performers, as in this excerpt by Deborah Jowitt (2008, 3) about dancer Damian Woetzel of the New York City Ballet:

   > He excels at the sprightly, the witty, the all-American. . . . At his farewell performance . . . he inhabited his role in *Fancy Free* with all the requisite braggadocio and naiveté. Seldom has the New York skyline looked as intoxicatingly big as it did to his sailor on leave, and never have I seen the barroom duet . . . look so increasingly tender and—in a questioning and exploratory way—so sexy.

Jowitt makes an evaluative comment ("excels at the sprightly") and backs it up with description of specific movements and their expressive qualities.

2. At other times, the choreography is the subject of evaluation. Here, Claudia La Rocco (2008, 1-2) discusses a performance by the Hubbard Street Dance Company:

   > Mr. Duato's "Gnawa" is a handsome dance, but predictably formulaic in its evocation of what the program notes call the Mediterranean's "spirituality and organic rhythms." Still, "Gnawa" is worth seeing for the percussive, haunting mix of North African and Spanish songs, and for the choreography's striking group patterns, infused with echoes of flamenco and various earthy folk-dance touches. If only Mr. Duato would ease up on the ambiance, and dig a little deeper.

La Rocco describes and analyzes what was problematic about the dance: It was "predictably formulaic," too heavy on ambiance, and too light on substance for her taste.

Likewise, if you come across a dance that you found unsuccessful or uninspiring, you should give specific reasons for your opinion. Conversely, if you found a dance successful or compelling, tell the reader why that was so.

Putting It Together

Although they are discussed as four separate ideas, description, analysis, interpretation, and evaluation are thoroughly interwoven in dance criticism. According to professional critics, the most emphasized of these is description. Each of the other modes is dependent on description for support and clarification, so it stands to reason that description should make up the main substance of your paper. This also underscores how important it is to be able to accurately and vividly communicate what you see onstage through your writing.

Use of Language

You have now read about the elements of a critique and have some ideas about the content of your paper. How can you best express these ideas? We have already discussed the importance of description in a critique. Critic David Vaughn (Meltzer 1979, 38) discusses his view on the specificity necessary for dance writing:

> You have to train yourself to write as vividly as possible in that immediate way that can conjure up an image to the reader. There's so much dance criticism that's written with words that don't really tell you what the movement is. It's like the English form of criticism where they'll say, "She was an enchanting Aurora with true ballerina radiance," which doesn't say a damn thing about the way she dances.

A purpose for description is evocation—to re-create some aspects of the performance for the reader. Critic Elizabeth Zimmer offers some insights that assist in the process of evocation. She advocates strong nouns, vibrant adjectives, and actions verbs like *lunge, squat, skim,* or *slice,* which conjure up mental images of action. Zimmer also cautions against using words like *graceful* or *beautiful,* suggesting instead that a writer find what actually happened that created that impression. She says, "Learn how to manipulate language that is genuinely expressive (Oliver 1991)."

Similes and Metaphors

Similes and metaphors help to communicate the impact of the work in an engaging way. Similes are expressions that compare one thing to another; they usually begin with *like* or *as.* Metaphors substitute one thing for another, implying a comparison rather than stating it overtly. Here are some examples from professional dance reviews.

Similes

Wearing black and gray leotards and tights, and pale makeup that doesn't outline eyes or lips, they walk in short, gliding steps, looking in Jennifer Tipton's cool lighting, like androids performing inexplicable tasks. (Jowitt 2004, 76)

. . .she sank to the floor, one leg beautifully stretched in front of her, and folded her body and arms forward like a dying swan. (Siegel 1976, 195)

Metaphors

Leslie Browne as the Wili queen was a wonder of danced fury, building from a deceptively quiet start into an explosion of leaps and turns . . . (Kisselgoff 1991, C3)

Heidi Latsky's "Summer Dance Riot," performed in a stifling black-box space with no more floor footage than a walk-in closet, was essentially a cabaret of much bizarreness and occasional charm. (Tobias 2004, 76)

Tense

Present tense is immediate and brings you close to the action. Past tense gives the sense that you have studied the performance in question. Either is appropriate for a dance review, but take care not to mix them inadvertently because it can be confusing.

Avoid the conditional tense (verbs preceded by *would* or *could*) unless it is truly needed for the sense of your sentence. The conditional tends to make the reader more removed from the action than simple past or present tense.

- **Present:** The dancer leaps and spins furiously across the stage.
- **Past:** The dancer leapt and spun furiously across the stage.
- **Conditional:** The dancer would leap and spin furiously across the stage.

Voice

First person (*I*, *we*) is conversational because it brings the reader into direct verbal contact with the writer. Second person (*you*) is also direct but is usually inappropriate for a formal paper. Third person (*he*, *she*, *it*) is slightly removed from the action. Professional critics use either first or third person; either can be a good choice for a response paper. Once again, don't mix them without cause.

- **First person:** I found the second dance too long.
- **Third person:** The second dance was too long.

If you choose first person, avoid starting sentences repeatedly with *I feel* or *I think*; the reader will assume that these are your thoughts and feelings without your repeatedly stating it.

Revision

Because writing is rarely perfect the first time around, you will find that it is important to write more than one draft. Composition texts suggest that after writing your first draft, you should check your paper for its flow as a whole, including transitions, topic sentences, introduction, and conclusion. When writing dance criticism, consider vivid language, consistent tense, interesting syntax, creativity of thought and language, and soundness of interpretations and evaluations.

Reader Review

Writing instructors such as Peter Elbow believe that it is very helpful to get an "outside eye" to read and respond to your writing, because

Reviewing Checklist for Dance Critiques

Following is a list of questions and considerations that can be used by a reader (and by writers themselves) in the revision process.

1. Does the critique give general information concerning date, place, and who is performing?

   _____

2. Are choreographers and composers named for each dance discussed? If soloists are discussed, are they named?

   _____

3. Does the critique include some description, analysis, interpretation, and evaluation, with an emphasis on description?

   _____

4. Is there a thesis statement for the paper as a whole?

   _____

5. Is there a thesis statement for each dance discussed?

   _____

6. Is there at least one "movement moment" in the paper?

   _____

7. Are interpretations and evaluations supported with description?

   _____

8. Are personal opinions explained?

   _____

9. Are there any errors in spelling, grammar, or punctuation? Are there any typing errors? Remember that spell check does not catch all errors (e.g. using _there_ instead of _their_).

   _____

10. Is punctuation used appropriately? Is there a comma where you would pause in reading aloud?

    _____

11. Is there variety in the texture of the sentences (length, complexity, type of punctuation, syntax)?

    _____

12. Does the paper flow as a whole? Is it interesting to read?

    _____

From W. Oliver, 2010, _Writing About Dance_ (Champaign, IL: Human Kinetics).

that reader will be able to point out areas of weakness. A reader who did not attend the performance that you have critiqued will be the best judge of the clarity of the paper. The reader should also note mechanical errors such as spelling and punctuation.

Final Draft

Based on readers' comments and any further observations of your own, make your final revisions and proofread your final draft before printing it out. Again, keep in mind that spell check does not catch all errors. Double-space your paper so your teacher will have room to write comments. Save a copy of the paper on your computer.

Rubrics for Dance Critiques

A rubric is a way of explicitly stating expectations for achievement in writing assignments. It is based on several specific attributes that are each rated separately as excellent, good, adequate, or poor; these separate ratings are then compiled for the total evaluation. Rubrics are useful because when you know the specific criteria by which papers are graded, you are more likely to do a good job with the assignment. Teachers may add to or modify the rubrics if desired. The eight elements in the rubric for dance critiques (see table 4.1) are explained briefly here:

   I. *Introduction* includes a context for the critique and an interesting assertion about the performance.
   II. *Identifying information* of company, choreographers, composers, directors, designers, dance titles, and dancers as appropriate.
   III. There is a *thesis statement* for the paper as a whole and for each dance discussed.
   IV. *Description* is vivid; it gives both a general sense of each dance and some specific movement moments.
   V. *Analysis, interpretation, and evaluation* are all present; interpretations and evaluations are supported by concrete observations.
   VI. Paper *flows* smoothly and maintains reader's interest.
   VII. *Conclusion* ties the paper together.
   VIII. *Conventions of English language* are followed accurately.

Table 4.1 Rubric for Dance Critiques

Expectation	Level 4	Level 3	Level 2	Level 1
Introduction	Gives a context for critique and an interesting assertion about the performance that captures the reader's attention.	Gives a context and a somewhat interesting assertion.	Gives a context without an assertion or vice versa.	Lacks a clear beginning altogether.
Identifying information	Identifies all choreographers, dance titles, composers, and so on, as necessary for the pieces reviewed; does not overidentify by listing every name in the entire program.	Identifies most of the key people necessary for pieces reviewed.	Identifies some of the key people necessary for pieces reviewed.	There is minimal identification.
Thesis statement for paper and each dance	Provides strong thesis statement for paper as a whole and each dance.	Provides thesis statement for paper and each dance; some are strong.	Lacks thesis statements for paper or some dances, or provides weak ones.	Lacks thesis statement for paper or any dance discussed.
Description	Gives lively general description and a great deal of vivid description of actual movement moments.	Gives good general description and some good description of actual movement moments.	Gives general description and some description of actual movement moments.	Gives general description but little or no description of actual movement moments.
Analysis, interpretation, evaluation	Includes analysis, interpretation, and evaluation; each is well supported by concrete observations of the dance itself; all opinions are supported.	Includes analysis, interpretation, and evaluation; most statements are supported by concrete observations.	Includes some of the three; statements are partially supported.	Includes little analysis or interpretation; statements and opinions are not supported.

Expectation	Level 4	Level 3	Level 2	Level 1
Flow	Maintains excellent flow because the discussion of each dance relates to its thesis sentence; thoughts follow logically; syntax is varied.	Maintains good flow because the discussion of each dance is usually related to its thesis sentence; thoughts usually follow logically; syntax is varied.	Maintains some flow; the discussion of each dance is somewhat unfocused; thoughts sometimes follow logically; syntax is somewhat varied.	Lacks flow; the discussion of each dance is unfocused and not logical; syntax is problematic.
Conclusion	Summarizes the writer's observations in an interesting way; adds something new.	Summarizes the writer's observations and may also add something new.	Partially summarizes the writer's observations.	Lacks clarity.
Conventions of English language	0-2 errors in spelling, punctuation, and grammar.	3-5 errors in spelling, punctuation, and grammar.	6-8 errors in spelling, punctuation, and grammar .	More than 8 errors in spelling, punctuation, and grammar.

Sample Critique

The vivid description in this student critique makes it exceptional. It also includes a strong introduction and conclusion; grounded analysis, interpretation, and evaluation; strong flow, and appropriate use of language conventions. The writer was able to create a strong thesis for the entire paper as well as thesis sentences for individual dances.

STREB

Jeanette Gentile, Providence College

Seven members of Streb Extreme Action performed in Rhode Island this Saturday, October 14, 2006, at the Providence Performing Arts Center in the production titled *Wild Blue Yonder*. The performance featured eleven unique and nerve-wracking pieces that each presented a different aspect of the sheer power of gravity and the human body.

The company's show could bedazzle nondancers and dancers alike; there is nothing intimidating or stuffy about it. Popular hits from several different decades play before the show and during intermissions. The set credited to Michael Casselli calls attention to a red and blue color scheme and an interesting arrangement of jumbled equipment, including poles, scaffolding, and various machines placed about the stage. The performers are not distinguished by their gender through their costuming; they all wear a series of sports tights and fitted shirts in dark, solid colors, with various colored or white crescent slashes. Shelly Sabel's vivid lighting and Aaron Henderson's video projections create visual effects that change for and within each number and morph between them, sending bright-colored shapes, letters, numbers, drawings, photographs, and colors dancing across the huge screen at the back of the stage. None of these theatrical elements, however, detracts from Streb's dedication to plain action or to commanding, unswerving moves that happened at the speed necessary to accomplish a given task.

The opening piece, "Orbit," features two dancers, roped and harnessed, that fly around the tall pole to which they are connected at center stage. The bodies become free-flowing and unrestricted as they intersect creatively as their supporting

Streb, Layers with Wheel.
Photo by Tom Caravaglia. Courtesy of Streb/Ringside Inc.

ropes coil about the pole. They float and swim through the air in slow motion, as if they were in a giant pool of water. The two simply lie supine on air, swinging farther and farther from the pole as their ropes unwind and they gracefully soar above the stage; the performers defy gravity on almost all levels. The camera located at the top of the pole magnifies the aerial view of the performers, illustrating their control, fearlessness, and precision while soaring through the air.

Another piece, "Moon," is also an extended thought-provoking ploy about gravity. Six people perform lying down on a blue floor while an overhead camera projects their images on the giant screen behind them; the live feed of moving dancers lying down on the blue floor, when projected vertically on the back wall, creates gravitational confusion. The ground seems frictionless against their slippery unitards and the bodies slide effortlessly across the surface. At first, the scene is baffling: The bodies resemble amoebas that are blubbering about under an electron microscope. However, as the work progresses, humor becomes visible and the images are comprehended. When the dancers crunch and creep along the floor, feet braced against its back edge, their images walk awkwardly erect on the wall. Their laborious exercises produce impossible, deceptive acts such as athletes forming wobbly human pyramids; standing or head-balancing on a partner's single, upraised hand; or flying upward with no apparent source of propulsion. The image of a gravity-free world is one that is difficult to imitate, yet Streb does the near impossible, per usual.

In the opening dance of the second half, "Ricochet," not only do performers repeatedly run forward and launch themselves against a large, transparent pane of clear plastic, but they also press against it, slide down, and mash their faces into the kind of extreme distortions that are unseen in face-to-floor impact. The dancers slam into the Plexiglass wall like birds flying into a bay window; the Plexiglass is amplified to stress the impact, but the impact cannot go unnoticed by any living being with the capability of vision in the theater.

Another piece that was particularly astounding was "Ripple." This work features performers venturing across a stretched truck strap. The dancers dive, run, hop, leap, and bend over around and under the strap; they even walk on it as if it were a tightrope at the top of a circus tent. The men and women can jump on independently, perch a second, and jump off, which ultimately leads to a horde of crazy racing fumbles. At another point in the dance, Streb may have intended to poke fun at ballet's courtly assists, which is exemplified during the "Rose Adagio" in the ballet *Sleeping Beauty*. Four people rotate a female dancer balanced atop the strap in a ballet attitude until her leg unfolds into a balanced, straight, vertical arabesque. But then the rest of the dancers fall facefirst onto the mat, not a typical ending for Sleeping Beauty's suitors. This work is yet another example of a witty and imaginative blend of dance, circus, and extreme sports. The strap appears to barely move as the performers maneuver on and off it, but at each human impact, video cameras set up near its end project on the back screen a vivid frenzy of vibration. The visual effect presents the impact as primitively as it's actually happening experientially in the dancers' bodies. Additionally, the audible noises the dancers make as they slam into the strap all at once and hit the floor beneath it convey impact pretty expressively.

The most crystal-clear memory of this show was that the dancers fell down—very hard and from very high. The company essentially toyed with physics: fighting and illustrating the laws of motion and gravity. Dancers bounced over and on one another, pulled each other with ropes, jumped into Plexiglass, hung from hoops, and slid across surfaces. The performers yelled cues and thudded onto mats. There was nothing fake or abstract about this show. Everything was real. The work that Streb does is labeled dance, but it is also something more than that. It is physical brute strength and power against the rules of nature. She pushes herself and her dancers right to the very edge; furthermore, she pushes her audience members there, too. With this performance, Streb has made her point. These dancers are pioneers and champions; even as they thrill the audience with spectacle and theatricality, they are testing what human beings can accomplish.

Wrap-Up

Writing dance critiques develops your critical-thinking skills and aesthetic judgment, or taste. To do criticism well, you need to describe, analyze, interpret, and evaluate dance performances, as shown in figure 4.1. Throughout this chapter are examples of how professional dance critics do these four things in their writing. Before the writing process can begin, you must take good notes on the performance that you attend; these notes serve as the starting point for free writing. Out of free writing come your introduction and thesis and your selection of which dances to write about. For each dance you discuss, find and highlight its outstanding features with vivid, action-packed language. Finally, tie your paper together with a conclusion, and consult the Reviewing Checklist for Dance Critiques on page 92. The rubric on page 94 can serve as a guide for excellence in your paper.

5

Dance Essays

The term essay is often used as a synonym for *paper*. An essay is a short literary composition on a single subject, usually presenting the personal view of the author. Essays are centered on the main points that the author wants to make; they inform, entertain, analyze, interpret, evaluate, persuade, or do any combination of these. In this book, we'll look at persuasive essays and reading analysis essays.

Persuasive Essay on Dance: What Do You Believe?

One type of essay is the *persuasive essay*, which expresses an opinion and attempts to convince the reader that said opinion is correct. For example, you may believe that dance should be an element of every child's education. A good essay on this topic will include the reasons for your belief and eloquently persuade the reader to agree with your viewpoint. Your passion about the topic, supported by evidence, logic, and strong writing, will make a winning essay.

Writing a persuasive essay improves your argumentation and writing skills by requiring you to take a stand and support it. It also develops your critical-thinking skills because in order to construct an argument, you have to first understand your topic and focus it appropriately. Finally, this type of writing gives you a chance to explore your own beliefs regarding dance issues. Although any paper you write involves some individual expression, a persuasive essay is probably the most personally expressive of any formal paper, since it incorporates your understanding, attitudes, and beliefs.

Two topics of persuasive essays are philosophical and editorial. The structure for both is the same; the differences between them concern the subject of the essays. A philosophical essay examines ideas concerning the nature of dance. Topics might include attempting to define what makes a dance good or how dance fundamentally differs from an aesthetic sport such as gymnastics. An editorial dance essay or opinion paper looks at a particular issue of concern in the contemporary dance world and offers a well-supported opinion or clarifying discussion on that matter. These topics might include the treatment of men in dance, how grant money is dispersed among choreographers, or whether dance in the public schools should be federally mandated. Editorial essays are similar in style to editorials in a newspaper.

No matter which type of persuasive essay you choose to write, the topic needs to be focused through the use of a guiding question, which is a question or series of questions examining a particular aspect of the topic. Like your topic, these questions may be generated by either the student or the teacher. Although both types of persuasive essays—philosophical and editorial—may be written with the same basic structure and approach, let's look at each separately for ideas about content.

Philosophical Dance Essay

Writing a philosophical essay deepens your understanding of what dance is and is not. It necessitates careful thinking about the qualities and properties of dance that distinguish it from anything else in the universe. It brings students into dialogue with questions that have been discussed by historical or contemporary philosophers and ultimately requires student writers to take a position.

Philosophical questions cannot be answered easily; instead they must be investigated logically. The philosophical essay takes the reader along for the ride as the writer explains his or her thought process and beliefs. Starting with the question, the writer then ponders various answers and their pitfalls before settling on the one that best addresses the initial query. Although only one guiding question is listed for each of the following topics, it is certainly possible to create others.

Sample Topics and Guiding Questions for Philosophical Essays

1. *Topic: defining dance.* Guiding question: What is dance? Is there a definition of dance that encompasses all of the types of dance around the world?

2. *Topic: beauty in dance.* Guiding question: What makes a dance beautiful? Is it totally subjective, or is there some element that can be identified as common to beautiful dances, at least within a given culture?

3. *Topic: functions of dance.* Guiding question: What are some of the functions of dance in society? Which of these functions is most important in your opinion, and why?

4. *Topic: dance and gymnastics.* Guiding question: What is the difference between dance and an aesthetic sport such as gymnastics or figure skating, and why and how are these differences significant?

5. *Topic: art and entertainment.* Guiding question: Do you make a distinction between dance as an art form and dance that entertains? Why or why not? If so, what distinguishes them from one another?

Editorial Dance Essay

Just like an editorial in a newspaper or on a news Web site, the dance editorial addresses a timely issue and gives an insightful analysis that helps to shape the opinions and actions of those who read it. Like the critical and philosophical essays, the editorial essay helps the writer to shape his or her opinion during the act of writing. Sharing your opinion about a particular dance issue can be enjoyable and also has the potential to effect change.

Sample Topics and Guiding Questions for Editorial Dance Essays

1. *Topic: men in dance.* Guiding question: In the typical ballet, modern, or jazz class, there are only a few men. Why are there so few men compared to women involved in dance in the United States? Is this a problem? If so, what can be done about it? Are men and women treated differently in the dance world?

2. *Topic: dance in public schools.* Guiding question: Should dance in the public schools be federally mandated? Why or why not? What would it mean if dance were in every public school?

3. *Topic: your favorite kinds of dance.* Guiding question: What are your favorite kinds of dance, and why?

4. *Topic: physical appearance.* Guiding question: How important is physical appearance (as opposed to dancing ability) in the professional dance world? Do you agree with the prevailing attitude? Why or why not?

5. *Topic: top choreographers.* Guiding question: In your opinion, who are three of the top choreographers working today, and why?

A topic, like men in dance, and a good guiding question can help the writer shape his or her opinion in an editorial dance eessay.

David DuBois of Newport, RI. Island Moving Co.

Getting Started: Free Writing for Persuasive Essays

Select your topic and guiding question from those listed for a philosophical or editorial dance essay, or use one given by your instructor. If your teacher gives you a topic but not a guiding question, you should create your own guiding question, designed like the ones given previously. Choose a question that truly interests you so that you can be fully engaged in writing the answer.

Using a guiding question as the starting point for your essay, free-write your responses first, using the same technique described in chapter 3. Writing answers to the questions in your guiding question is the jumping-off point for an exploration of your topic and will help you develop your point of view. As explained in chapter 4, do not worry about your organization, grammar, or clarity at this point in your process. You are simply putting your thoughts on paper.

Purpose and Audience

After free writing, but before you begin to shape your paper, you need to think about why you are writing and for whom. Most likely, you are writing this paper because it is a class assignment, but beyond that, you are writing to inform yourself and your audience about a topic and your opinion about it. Clearly, it is important to select a topic that is of personal interest to you because it is your excitement about the topic that will engage your audience.

Think of your peers or classmates as your audience, unless your instructor tells you otherwise. This will help you determine how much background information, or context, is needed in discussing your topic as well as which terminology might need clarification. Imagine presenting this paper to your class, and think about the ways in which you can make your ideas clear and interesting. If you are writing an editorial essay, imagine how it might look published on the editorial page of your student newspaper. In fact, if it turns out well, why not submit it to your school paper for publication?

Creating a Thesis

Writing an essay or almost any paper requires that you construct a thesis, which is usually found in the first two paragraphs of your paper. As noted in chapter 4, a thesis is the core assertion in your paper that informs your reader about your point of view on a particular topic. In your free writing, you responded to questions posed in your guiding question. The central response to the guiding question then becomes the key to your thesis. Another way to think of this is to ask yourself this question: What is the most important idea to emerge in my free writing? This idea can serve as the first draft of your thesis statement. You may not be able to clearly articulate your thesis until you have written a draft of your paper; however, the process of organizing and writing down your thoughts will help you clarify your opinions.

Here is an example of a topic, guiding question, and thesis and its improvement. The student chose an *editorial* essay, one in which expressing her opinion about the subject was the foremost concern. The topic was mirrors in the dance class, and her guiding question was *Do mirrors in the dance class have a positive or negative effect on students?*

Her thesis (and the answer to the guiding question) was *The constant use of mirrors in the dance class is bad for students*. This statement is good because the student has answered the guiding question and given us her viewpoint, but there is not enough information about why there is a problem.

The second draft of her thesis was *The constant use of mirrors in the dance class is bad for students because it can create problems with self-esteem and cause an overreliance on visual feedback*. This version is better because it includes both the author's viewpoint and two specific reasons for the problem.

Writers often place the thesis in the first paragraph, but not always. The thesis may need quite a bit of context in order to make sense; in that case, placing it in the first paragraph would be premature.

Title

Make sure to give your paper a meaningful title, preferably one that shows your point of view on the subject. For a paper on male dancers, a student titled his paper "Male Dancers: Shunned by Society." For a paper on eating disorders among dancers, a student titled her paper "A Call for Action for the Dancing World." You might need to wait until after your first draft is written before naming your paper in order to have a better-developed idea about your subject.

Introduction

An opening paragraph should tell the reader something about the topic at hand, arouse curiosity about that subject, and give us the author's attitude toward the subject. Many good introductions open with a statement about the general subject, then limit or focus the subject in some way, and finally deliver the thesis statement, which states the writer's main point. An introduction may also begin with a quotation, an anecdote, a comparison, or a strong opinion.

Here is an example of an opening of an essay that arouses the reader's curiosity. Choreographer Bill T. Jones (1997, n.p.) opens with an anecdote in his editorial titled "You Don't Have to Be Thin to Dance."

> At a recent dinner, I was seated next to a fashion designer who, speaking triumphantly of his new diet, joked that he was turning into a prominent dancer for the New York City Ballet who is noted for being painfully thin. This anecdote is useful in leading us into a discussion of body image in contemporary dance.

This opening sentence makes the reader curious about the fashion designer and his diet and how that will tie in the with author's topic, which is mentioned in the second sentence.

In this essay, dancer and choreographer Martha Graham (1998, 50) states her thesis in the first paragraph:

> Throughout time dance has not changed in one essential function. The function of the dance is communication. The responsibility that dance fulfill its function belongs to us who are dancing today.

She opens with a sentence that gives a context for her essay, and then goes straight to her main point. Both the second and third sentences make up her thesis.

Developing Your Argument and Conclusion

After writing a thesis statement (with the understanding that it may change as your paper develops) and your introduction, you need to develop your arguments. The main goal of your essay is to convince the reader that your analysis and opinion are valid. You do this by using your powers of reasoning to make arguments that support your thesis statement. For instance, if you believe that dance in the public schools should be federally mandated, give at least three good reasons. Each reason should be discussed in one or more paragraphs. After making your arguments, summarize your points in your paper's conclusion and offer a recommendation or a new insight. Be as convincing as possible in order to win readers over to your point of view.

Following is a sample conclusion by a student on why dance should be federally mandated in the public schools:

> Finally, by federally mandating dance in the public school system, an improvement in the overall welfare of students is possible. The physical health of students would improve as they conditioned their bodies daily and learned discipline. Students would become more culturally aware by taking dance classes that teach them about the historical roots of the dances they learn and about their own cultures, which have roots in dance. Students' mental health would be strengthened, since dance can release stress and convey personal expression. Dance classes would allow creativity to flourish. Without federal mandates, there is no way to ensure that structured dance classes or programs would be offered at all public schools. It is important that dance be federally mandated so that students receive all of the benefits of dance and the adults of our future are physically and mentally healthy, culturally aware, and well rounded (Kraus, Hilsendager, & Dixon 1990).

References

In developing your arguments, you may elect to use references that support your position. These include books, editorials, journal and magazine articles, reputable Web sites, and interviews. Make sure the support comes from experts in the field. Using references will tend to make your paper longer and a little more complex. If you do use references, don't lose your own voice. The idea is to use the references to support your own ideas rather than supplant them. The dance essay should focus on your thoughts and opinions rather than the ideas of other people. For a five-page essay, about three or four references are adequate. A very short essay (fewer than three pages) may not require references, but consult your teacher for guidelines. If you already know quite a bit about the selected topic, you may not need references; if the topic is somewhat new to you, references may be necessary.

Be sure to give appropriate credit for quotations and any ideas (other than your own) that are not common knowledge. Common knowledge is information that is found in at least three sources or something that most people would know. See page 140 in chapter 6 for further information on citations and references.

Structure

The following sample structure may be modified depending on the length of your essay. A longer essay may require more than one paragraph of background material before argumentation begins and will require more arguments. For this three-page essay, you may not need any sources, or you might use one or two.

Title (should reflect your viewpoint)

    I. Introduction

        A. Context and topic

        B. Thesis statement

    II. Body

        A. Argument 1

            1. Example

            2. Example

            3. Example

        B. Argument 2

            1. Example

            2. Example

            3. Example

        C. Argument 3

            1. Example

            2. Example

            3. Example

        D. Argument 4

            1. Example

            2. Example

            3. Example

   III. Conclusion

        A. Summary of arguments

        B. Restatement of opinion in a new way

Language

Usually in a philosophical or editorial essay, you do not need much movement description. However, you still need to use strong and evocative language in order to hold the reader's attention. Also important is the art of skillful argumentation; the act of persuasion through reasoned argument is the crux of your essay and is best accomplished by writing clearly and logically, making it easy for the reader to follow you from one thought to the next.

Following is an excerpt from a student essay on dance as a form of expression. It makes a strong statement in the opening phrase of the first sentence and then elaborates on the idea in two different ways that clearly reinforce the original premise.

> Dance is an exposure of the human body in its most naked form, whether simply raising one's hand or performing a ballet. We can see the physical strengths and shortcomings of the human body through dance.

Here is the opening of a student essay that is printed in full at the end of the section. These opening lines evoke images in the mind's eye:

> The graceful lines of a ballet dancer's body are a stark contrast to the powerful movements of West African cultural dancers. The crisp steps of a tap dancer do not share much in common with the refined gestures of a modern dancer. However, each style of dance can be seen as beautiful and moving by those who watch it.

Revision

Have a friend read your paper aloud to you, and have him or her stop whenever something doesn't make sense. Discuss these spots with your friend, mark your paper, and come back to those places later to revise. Ask your friend if your arguments are convincing; if they are not, ask why.

Final Draft

Once you have received feedback, go back to your computer and incorporate the suggestions into your paper. Make sure that your

Checklist for Persuasive Essays on Dance

Following is a list of items that should appear in every persuasive essay on dance.

1. Opening paragraph gives some background information on the topic and piques the reader's interest.

2. Thesis makes a specific observation about the topic, which conveys your viewpoint about it.

3. Each argument has its own paragraph (unless you are writing a one-page essay) and is explained fully.

4. Each argument is supported with accurate evidence.

5. Writing centers on your own voice rather than the opinions or ideas of others.

6. Essay flows logically from one point to the next.

7. All paragraphs relate to the thesis statement.

8. Conclusion summarizes the main points and suggests a solution to the problem or points to a new way of looking at the issue.

9. References, if used, are properly cited.

10. Grammar, spelling, and punctuation are correct. Be aware of the limitations of spell check.

references, if any are used, have been properly cited. Carefully check grammar, punctuation, and spelling; remember that spell check does not catch everything (e.g., it doesn't know the difference between *their* and *there*).

A rubric is a way of explicitly stating expectations for achievement in writing assignments. It is based on specific attributes that are each rated separately as excellent, good, adequate, or poor; these separate ratings are then compiled for the total evaluation. Rubrics are useful because you are more likely to do a good job with an assignment when you know the specific criteria by which papers are graded. Teachers may add to or modify the rubrics if desired. There are six elements in the rubric for persuasive essays (see table 5.1), which are explained briefly here:

1. *Introduction* includes a context for the essay, a brief description of your topic, and your viewpoint.
2. *Thesis statement* indicates topic and an original insight or assertion.
3. *Ideas and development* include at least three specific arguments that are logical and supported by specific examples, along with your perspective.
4. Paper *flows* smoothly and logically while maintaining reader's interest.
5. *Conclusion* ties the paper together and offers a recommendation or new insight.
6. *Conventions of English language* are followed.

Sample Persuasive Essay

This student essay starts by stressing the amazing variety of styles in dance, which link to her thesis at the end of the first paragraph. The body of her paper discusses some dance elements that contribute to the idea of beauty, including strong choreography, communication, passion, and talent. Her conclusion returns to the original point that beauty cannot be defined in one particular way, and adds that each of the four qualities discussed is important in judging what is beautiful. The concepts are conveyed well through a clear structure, appropriate use of quotations, and a logical flow of ideas.

BEAUTY IN DANCE

Courtney Rogers, Providence College

The graceful lines of a ballet dancer's body are a stark contrast to the powerful movements of West African cultural dancers. The crisp steps of a tap dancer do not share much in common with the refined gestures of a modern dancer. However, each style of dance can be seen as beautiful and moving by those who watch it. One single person is capable of seeing each type of dance and enjoying it equally, despite the differences in movement and presentation. Beauty can be seen in the expression

Table 5.1 Rubric for Persuasive Essay

Expectation	Level 4	Level 3	Level 2	Level 1
Introduction	Gives context, identifies topic, and fully engages reader's attention.	Gives context, identifies topic, and engages reader's attention.	Lacks either context or clear topic and only partially engages reader's attention.	Lacks clear beginning altogether.
Thesis statement	Gives good indication of topic, offers an original insight, and indicates writer's attitude.	Gives good indication of both topic and writer's attitude.	Gives some indication of topic or writer's attitude.	Lacks thesis or gives little indication of topic or writer's attitude.
Ideas and development	Arguments that support thesis are accurate and relevant; arguments are always supported with evidence.	Arguments that support thesis are accurate and relevant; arguments are usually supported with evidence.	Some arguments are given but are not always accurate or relevant; arguments are sometimes supported with evidence.	Arguments are not given for writer's assertion, or those given do not make sense.
Flow	Each paragraph relates to its topic sentence; thoughts flow logically; transitions between paragraphs are smooth; syntax is varied; language is interesting.	Each paragraph relates to its topic sentence; thoughts usually flow logically; transitions between paragraphs are often smooth; syntax is varied.	Each paragraph usually relates to its topic sentence; thoughts sometimes flow logically; syntax is sometimes repetitive or confusing.	Paragraphs are disorganized and illogical; syntax is problematic.
Conclusion	Summarizes writer's observations in an interesting way; adds something new.	Summarizes writer's observations and may also add something new.	Partially summarizes writer's observations.	Lacks clarity or no conclusion is offered.
Conventions of English language	0-2 errors in spelling, punctuation, and grammar.	3-5 errors in spelling, punctuation, and grammar.	6-8 errors in spelling, punctuation, and grammar.	More than 8 errors in spelling, punctuation, and grammar.

of abstract dances, dances with story lines and pantomimes, and cultural dances. "Expressiveness is not a single, uniform power" (Highwater 136). This being said, there is no one correct definition of a beautiful dance. The expression and passion in dance are what make it beautiful, and it can be said that beauty in dance is almost entirely subjective.

Strong choreography is one aspect of dance that makes it beautiful. Rarely would one enjoy a dance that was badly choreographed. The way the dancers work together on stage with the choreography is very important. If the performers do not move together when they are supposed to, or do not move separately when they are supposed to, the concept the choreographer intended to portray will not come across to the audience. Hence, here is the subjective aspect of dance. If members of the audience do not understand what they are

Choreography and the way dancers move together
can evoke a sense of beauty in dance.

Alvin Ailey American Dance Theater in Alvin Ailey's *Revelations*.
Photo by Andrew Eccles.

seeing, it will be difficult for them to see beauty in the dance, or even enjoy the dance, if they are just simply trying to figure out what is happening the entire time.

In the same way, the audience must be able to relate to the dance that they are viewing. "The usual intention of dancing—and that includes abstract dance despite its claims of ambiguity—is to depict what is before us and what is happening to us" (Highwater 186). This point may have some cultural aspects to it as well. For example, an American person viewing an East Indian dance for the first time may not be able to relate to the concepts presented. So, while he or she may see the beautiful costumes and enjoy the music, the actual beauty in the dance itself may be lost. However, after gaining a greater understanding of India's cultural history or viewing more Indian dancing, the audience member may come to a better appreciation of the beauty of the entire dance culturally.

Perhaps the most important aspect of a beautiful dance is the emotion and passion portrayed by the performers. When a dancer is good at what she does, and her enjoyment is clearly visible to the audience, it makes for a more gratifying experience for everyone. There has to be life behind the dancers' movements, or "fire in the eyes," so to speak. A talented dancer without passion for what she does can be singled out on stage, even by an untrained eye. "The feeling of a movement will appear when that movement is danced, because that's where the life is. The life does not lie outside the dancing, however strange or non-strange, conventional or non-conventional the dancing is, the life of a dance lies there (Highwater 189).

However, some form of talent must also be present in order for a dance to be widely considered beautiful. All of the passion in the world could not make an untrained, untalented dancer beautiful on the stage next to talented, trained dancers. Once again, subjectivity is a factor here as well. Television shows such as *So You Think You Can Dance* have proven that what one person sees as beautiful dancing another person could see as awkward flailing and jumping. Insight into the dance world can help to better differentiate between what is truly beautiful and what is not. Dance is more than just random movements put on stage to entertain an audience. The movements "are not momentary outbursts of passion—they reveal a deep human grasp of unity and continuity" (Highwater 137).

Subjectivity is definitely one of the major difficulties in defining what is beautiful and what is not beautiful in dance. In today's society, "people are being presented with a constantly increasing number of ways to think of, look at, and evaluate the same thing" (Highwater 137). We value individualism and independent thinking, so a complete consensus on a definition as abstract as "beauty" is almost impossible. Technically, every single person could have a definition of what is beautiful, and each could be correct, since it is his opinion from his own perspective. However, these standards of choreography, passion, talent, and connection with the audience help to better define beauty in dance.

Works Cited

Highwater, Jamake. 1992. *Dance: Rituals of experience*. Hightstown, NJ: Princeton Books.

Reading Analysis Paper and Book Review

In writing this type of paper, you are doing two things: summarizing the readings and offering your analysis and evaluation. The first task for each reading is to understand what the author is saying; the second task is to discover what you make of it. Your audience should come away with a sense of what the reading is about, how you responded to it, and why. A reading analysis paper discusses one or more articles or book chapters. A book review examines an entire book, and it gives a supported opinion of the value of the book. The summary paper exercise in chapter 3, page 62, is good preparation for writing these two kinds of papers.

Reading Analysis Paper

Reading analysis papers (also known as response papers) are similar to persuasive essays in that they share your viewpoint with the reader. However, instead of centering primarily on a thesis, or one particular point that you are trying to make, this paper explores different aspects of the reading and may make various points that aren't specifically related to one another.

For this kind of paper, students read one or more articles or chapters and then write about the readings. This paper requires summarizing, locating interesting or controversial ideas, and then responding to those ideas. Following are some things to keep in mind while writing:

1. What are the author's main points?
2. What is new for you in this reading?
3. Find a quotation or point that you find interesting, and comment on it.
4. What are the strengths and weaknesses of the author's ideas? Do you agree with the main points? Why or why not?
5. If you are writing about more than one article or chapter, what, if anything, ties them together?
6. Create a meaningful title that tells the reader something about the points you will make.
7. Your summary should take up about one-third of your paper; the rest of your paper should be your own response. The reader should be able to understand both the main points of each article and your opinions of them.
8. Suggested length is three to four pages, based on one to five articles or chapters (i.e., one very long reading, three medium length, or five short).

Getting Started: Free Writing for Reading Analysis Papers

Start by reading each article or chapter thoroughly, taking notes as you go. Jot down interesting points, new ideas, anything that you strongly agree or disagree with, observations about writing style, and questions that arise. Then, summarize each article or chapter in a few sentences each, making sure to include the name of the article and the author. Because the summary is so short, you will need to find and include only the most important ideas.

Next, think about the common themes or ideas among the articles. Write one or two sentences conveying these common ideas that can become the thesis for your paper. Since the purpose of this paper isn't to prove one particular point, your thesis can simply be an interesting assertion about the focus of the readings (see table 5.2 on p. 120).

Introduction

Your introduction will focus on the common themes among the articles you have read. If you are writing about one long chapter, briefly discuss the main theme and give it some context. You may also choose to include an attention getter, personal anecdote, or interesting observation in your opening paragraph.

Structure

Here are two possible choices for organizing the remainder of the paper:

1. All summaries first; critical discussion of selected issues next; conclusion
2. Summary of one article, followed immediately by critical discussion of that article; repeat for each article; conclusion

The advantage of the first structure is that the reader finds out more quickly about all of the articles you've read. This structure also allows students to focus on issues they are most interested in rather than respond in equal length to every article. The advantage of the second format is that you don't need to split the summary from the discussion of the article, allowing a smooth transition between ideas.

Option 1

Title (related to common theme among writings)

   I. Introduction

      A. Introduction of theme

      B. General thesis or assertion about readings

   II. Body

      A. Summaries

         1. Article 1

         2. Article 2

         3. Article 3

      B. Analysis

         1. Article 1

         2. Article 2

         3. Article 3

  III. Conclusion

Option 2

Title (related to common theme among readings)

   I. Introduction

    A. Introduction of theme

    B. General thesis or assertion about readings

II. Body

    A. Article 1

        1. Summary

        2. Analysis

    B. Article 2

        1. Summary

        2. Analysis

    C. Article 3

        1. Summary

        2. Analysis

III. Conclusion

Critical Analysis

Your job is to point out and comment on interesting or controversial issues, new ideas, and the author's effectiveness in conveying her or his point. Although you do not have the time or space in this paper to make a well-developed argument on an issue, each point you make should be supported in some way. A few short quotations should be included in this part of your paper. You may also use your personal experience as the basis for the analysis and evaluation of ideas.

Checklist for Reading Analysis Paper

1. Summarize each article. Each summary highlights the author's main point and includes the author's name and the title of the article.

2. Analyze a few points in the readings. This includes a recap of a particular point made by the author and then your interpretation and evaluation of that point. You may also critique the overall style or content of a reading.

3. Conclusion tells your audience your attitude toward the topic, now that you have explored these readings.

Table 5.2　Rubric for Reading Analysis Paper

Expectation	Level 4	Level 3	Level 2	Level 1
Introduction	Gives context, identifies topic, and fully engages reader's attention.	Gives context, identifies topic, and engages reader's attention.	Lacks either context or clear topic and partially engages reader's attention.	Lacks clear beginning altogether.
Identifying information	Identifies all authors and article titles.	Identifies most authors and titles.	Identifies some authors and titles.	Minimal identification.
Article Summaries	Provides accurate, concise summary for articles.	Provides accurate, concise summary for each article.	Provides summary for each article.	Missing summary, or summary is written in a very confusing way.
Analysis and response	Includes lively discussion of one or more issues from reading, using a brief quotation from each reading.	Includes discussion of one or more issues from reading, using a brief quotation from each reading.	Includes discussion of one or more issues from reading but may lack quotation, or discussion is unclear.	Includes discussion of one or more issues from reading but does not make coherent points; quotation is missing.
Attitude toward topic	Reveals attitude toward readings individually and topic as a whole in a compelling way.	Reveals attitude toward readings individually and topic as a whole in a coherent way.	Reveals attitude toward readings and topic in a somewhat coherent way.	Either reveals attitude toward readings incoherently or doesn't reveal attitude at all.
Flow	Each paragraph relates to its topic sentence; thoughts flow logically; transitions between paragraphs are smooth; syntax is varied; language is interesting.	Each paragraph relates to its topic sentence; thoughts usually flow logically; transitions between paragraphs are often smooth; syntax is varied.	Each paragraph usually relates to its topic sentence; thoughts sometimes flow logically; syntax is sometimes repetitive or confusing.	Paragraphs are disorganized and illogical; syntax is problematic.

Expectation	Level 4	Level 3	Level 2	Level 1
Conclusion	Summarizes the writer's observations in an interesting way; adds something new.	Summarizes the writer's observations and may also add something new.	Partially summarizes the writer's observations.	Lacks clarity or conclusion is not offered.
Conventions of English language	0-2 errors in spelling, punctuation, and grammar.	3-5 errors in spelling, punctuation, and grammar.	6-8 errors in spelling, punctuation, and grammar.	More than 8 errors in spelling, punctuation, and grammar.

Conclusion

What thoughts and feelings were you left with at the end of your reading? Briefly, let the reader know how the ideas you've discussed affected you, and tie it all together with a new thought or recommendation on the topic.

Sample Reading Analysis Paper

In this paper, the author's introduction opens with a metaphor about the dancer's body, which relates to the title of her paper and ties all of the readings together. Next, she presents a concise summary of each article, along with an interesting quotation that supports an important idea for each article. Her analysis begins on a personal note, linking her own experience to themes within the articles. She extends her discussion further by explaining her support for some of the authors' opinions, adding a few well-chosen quotations. She uses both logic and emotion to express her viewpoint; it is easy to follow her thoughts since they are both clearly written and highly engaging. She ends with a statement of belief that builds upon a focal point within the articles, and links back to her opening idea.

THE DANCER'S BODY: AN INSTRUMENT TO BE TREASURED

Alyssa Catjakis, Providence College

The painter has his brush to create paintings, and the pianist plays her piano to make music. The dancer's instrument, on the other hand, cannot be bought in a store or polished and put away for future use. The dancer *is* her own instrument; she uses her body to express her art form with mere motion. The articles written by Friedler and Glazer, Sandler, and Looseleaf are all concerned with matters of the body, especially with body image issues and the sensuality involved with dance.

Friedler and Glazer talk about the stereotypical dancer's body: "thin, delicate and vulnerable looking . . . She has long legs and arms, a compact torso, and small breasts" (177-178). Recently, though, directors and choreographers of modern dance tend to work with women who are stronger and more grounded. Because the dancer's body is so imperative to her art, factors like pregnancy and age can be a huge burden on a dancer's career. Still, many dancers work during and after their pregnancies, and many of the most eloquent dancers on stage are aging performers. Dancers use their bodies to express both their spirituality and sensuality. When dancers work together, relationships inevitably form—either platonically as with Doris Humphrey and Charles Weidman, or sexually as in Bob Fosse and Gwen Verdon's case. Today, audiences have finally become more accepting of dancer's bodies—young or old, thick or thin, tall or short.

Sandler writes about the fact that dancers are constantly being looked at. She proposes that body shape has nothing to do with what makes someone a dancer. The body is not merely an object but rather a "living, breathing subject (198). Our culture teaches us to objectify our bodies—ugly or sexy, fat or skinny; there is no 'miraculous life-sustaining'" (199) quality that is frequently seen in other cultures. Many dancers do not feel up to par with the media-driven notions of what a dancer is "supposed" to look like. We have somehow come to believe that it is fine for dancers to appear sexy but not hold any sexual power. But in reality, sexuality cannot be separated from dancing. Sandler calls us to reject the values forced on us by the media and to accept ourselves in our God-given form.

Looseleaf addresses the fact that the art of dance is undoubtedly connected with sexuality. But is it sexist to be sexy onstage? Linda Celeste Sims and Lorena Feijóo agree that to be a true artist is to understand what roles call for being sexy. In a world where sex is "used to sell everything from cars to cigarettes" (45), many dancers are using their sex appeal on TV, in movies, and onstage. Yena Glover believes that it's sexist only if you're using sexuality in dance to sell. Most agree that true sexiness comes from confidence, an immediate result of being comfortable with yourself in your own skin.

For years, I've experienced the need to fit the physical mold of the perfect dancer. As much as I hate to admit it, it is all too easy to submit to the misconstrued definition of beauty that our culture promotes. Envision a ballerina. Does she have wide-set hips and solid thighs? Doubtful. Does that mean that a woman with a fuller figure cannot practice ballet? Of course not. However, we have an archetype in our minds about what is supposed to be. It is unfortunate that this petty little stereotype can affect the self-esteem of not only dancers, but women in general around the world. It is especially difficult for dancers, though, because they are constantly being critiqued by directors and audiences. And as if that were not enough pressure, when they aren't onstage, they are practicing in front of the mirror at the studio, where they learn to be their own harshest critics. Dance is such a gorgeous artistic expression; dancers should feel just as beautiful as the art while they are performing.

In Friedler and Glazer's article, Jawole Willa Ja Zollar, director of the Urban Bush Women Company, says, "I like to see women feel good about their bodies. Women who have large breasts or big hips or thick thighs should feel that they can use those parts of themselves in dance" (179). I think this is the reason why I am becoming increasingly drawn to modern dance. I feel (at least so far in my limited exposure to it) that it is more about being connected with yourself and the world around you than it is about being a delicate object for audiences to gawk at. It's about using your body to express yourself, regardless of your size—or even technical ability for that matter. The circumference of my waist has no correlation to how well I can execute a pirouette. Before reading this article, I thought that the majority of the dance community adhered to the clichéd notion of what dancers should look like. It's comforting to know choreographers are celebrating the female form in all of its curvaceous beauty. Even more encouraging is that the world of modern dance has come to appreciate women for their talent and passion rather than for their shape and size.

Sandler makes an excellent observation about the narrow-mindedness of our nature. "We have been taught that one side, one group, one idea must win. If there is only one right way to look, then there is only one right way to be, and we all lose" (204). We live in a world of such objectivity—right or wrong, black or white, yes or no. But who has the authority to tell someone that they are not fit to dance? When I was younger, I took a ballet technique class with a girl named Samantha. Sam was about four years older than me, very heavy set, and not the most technically gifted dancer at the barre. Yet every week, Sam came to the studio with a smile on her face, ready to work hard and improve her technique. I will always be inspired by her determination and perseverance. She could have easily been discouraged from dancing as was the classmate Sandler mentions who was told she was too short to dance. All too often, we settle for the ideas of others. As Sandler's quote implies, we hear something that we've been told is right and we automatically agree; for instance, dancers are tall and thin. Thank goodness that we've had women to speak up and go against the grain. Where would we be without the optimistic, creative contributions of Isadora Duncan and Martha Graham who have pushed the boundaries with their own bodies?

If all dancers resembled the dainty stick figures we are all led to believe they should look like, the world of dance would be, quite frankly, pretty monotonous. Rather, the body should be seen as a sacred gift. We shouldn't criticize it for not meeting the outrageous unattainable standards that society has put forth. Rather, we must learn to appreciate the body for giving us the opportunity to dance—to physically convey to the world what our souls are yearning to share.

Works Cited

Friedler, Sharon, and Susan Glazer. 1997. Dancers talk about the physical body, theory and practice and using the knowledge. In *Dancing female*, eds. Friedler and Glazer. Amsterdam: Harwood.

Looseleaf, Victoria. 2008. Is it sexist to be sexy? *Dance Magazine*, July, 44-46.

Sandler, Julie. 1997. Standing in awe, sitting in judgment. In *Dancing female*, eds. Friedler and Glazer. Amsterdam: Harwood.

Book Review

A book review gives readers an overview of the book and discusses its strengths and weaknesses. Some dance books that lend themselves well to book reviews are autobiographies such as Allegra Kent's

Once a Dancer . . . (1997) or Paul Taylor's *Private Domain* (1999), and single-author books on a specific dance genre such as Constance Valis Hill's *Brotherhood in Rhythm* (2000) or *Sharing the Dance* by Cynthia Novak (1990). In a dance composition class, it can be interesting to review various composition textbooks and compare approaches. In a pedagogy class, the same idea could be applied to instructional books. In a technique or dance history class, students could each read a biography of a different choreographer, write a book review, and share the results. Critically considering a group of books as a class exposes the range of ideas within an area of dance. The benefits to students from writing book reviews are developing a deep knowledge of the content and developing a point of view about the book.

Here are some things to include in your book review:

- Author, title, and date of publication
- General statement about the subject and purpose of the book
- Overview of content or plot
- Main themes and ideas
- Interesting passages and how they affected you
- Description of writing style
- Illustrations, photos, and charts, if applicable
- Strengths and weaknesses (in conclusion section)
- Description of ideal audience for this book (describe in conclusion section)
- Suggested length of three pages

The list of things to keep in mind for reading analysis papers on page 117 also works for the book review.

Getting Started: Free Writing for Book Reviews

Take notes while reading the book; pay attention to both style and content. It is advisable to write a summary for each chapter to help you remember key ideas later in your process. Write down a few quotations that seem particularly noteworthy, along with their page numbers. It is best to read the book over a period of time (a week or two) rather than all at once (the night before your paper is due!). This allows more time to digest the material and begin thinking about ideas for your paper.

   Be sure to notice the structure of the book. How many chapters or sections are there, and what is their significance? How does the book progress? Does the structure make sense to you (see table 5.3 on p. 128)?

Introduction

The first paragraph includes an overview of the book and an assertion about it, which is your thesis statement. It also is a place for catching the reader's attention, perhaps with a quotation from the book. You also might try grabbing the reader's interest by finding the most outrageous things in the book and mentioning them here. Or you might share an idea that you found intellectually stimulating, emotionally powerful, or practical.

Structure

This format may be modified as necessary. For instance, you may have more examples for one point than for another. Also, some points may not need examples; for instance, when discussing charts or illustrations, it may be enough to simply mention them briefly.

Title

- I. Introduction
  - A. General overview of book, including who, what, when, where, and why
  - B. Thesis statement
- II. Body
  - A. Point 1
    1. Example
    2. Example
  - B. Point 2
    1. Example
    2. Example
  - C. Point 3
    1. Example
    2. Example
- III. Conclusion
  - A. Summary
  - B. Recommendation

Body

The body of the paper discusses themes and ideas, interesting passages, writing style, structure, and illustrations. Use adjectives to describe these elements in order to convey a sense of detail. Be sure to include at least one quotation or specific example from the book to illustrate a point that you make that is related to your thesis.

Conclusion

The conclusion in a book review might be longer than a paragraph, because it includes an analysis of the book's strengths and weaknesses. It ties back to your thesis statement and gives the reader specific reasons for your opinions. Your closing sentences include your overall opinion of the book and for whom it might be valuable or enjoyable.

Checklist for Book Review

1. Opening paragraph includes a general description: author, title, and date of publication.
2. Opening paragraph grabs the reader's attention and makes an assertion about the book.
3. Discuss the content, main ideas, plot (if applicable), and interesting ideas or subjects.
4. Discuss structure, writing style, and illustrations.
5. Discuss strengths and weaknesses.
6. Include at least one quotation.
7. Finish with a supported recommendation.

Table 5.3 Rubric for Book Review

Expectation	Level 4	Level 3	Level 2	Level 1
Introduction	Gives context; identifies author, title, and date; gives overview and thesis statement; fully engages reader's attention.	Gives context; identifies author, title, and date; gives overview and thesis statement; engages reader's attention.	Lacks either context, overview, thesis, or author and title information; only partially engages reader's attention.	Lacks clear beginning altogether.
Content of book	Discusses main ideas and other subject matter (and plot if applicable) in a clear and compelling way.	Discusses main ideas and other subject matter (and plot if applicable) in a clear way.	Discusses main ideas and other subject matter (and plot if applicable) in a somewhat clear way.	Discussion of main ideas lacks substance and clarity.
Style of book	Discusses very clearly the structure, writing style, illustrations, and any interesting features.	Discusses clearly the structure, writing style, illustrations, and any interesting features.	Discusses some but not all of structure, writing style, illustrations, and interesting features; or all are present but lack clarity.	Discussion touches only minimally if at all on structure, writing style, illustrations, and interesting features.
Conclusion	Identifies audience for book; evaluates book's strengths and weaknesses and links to thesis; and overall supports opinion in a compelling way.	Identifies audience for book; evaluates book's strengths and weaknesses and links to thesis; and overall supports opinion.	Identifies audience for book; evaluates book's strengths and weaknesses; link to thesis or support for opinion is weak or missing.	Conclusion is missing two or more elements or is omitted.
Quotations	At least one quotation is used very well to illustrate a point.	At least one quotation is used well to illustrate a point.	At least one quotation is used but is not appropriate to point.	Quotation is omitted.

Expectation	Level 4	Level 3	Level 2	Level 1
Flow	Each paragraph relates to its topic sentence; thoughts flow logically; transitions between paragraphs are smooth; syntax is varied; language is interesting.	Each paragraph relates to its topic sentence; thoughts usually flow logically; transitions between paragraphs are often smooth; syntax is varied.	Each paragraph usually relates to its topic sentence; thoughts sometimes flow logically; syntax is sometimes repetitive or confusing.	Paragraphs are disorganized and illogical; syntax is problematic.
Conventions of English language	0-2 errors in spelling, punctuation, and grammar.	3-5 errors in spelling, punctuation, and grammar.	6-8 errors in spelling, punctuation, and grammar.	More than 8 errors in spelling, punctuation, and grammar.

Sample Book Review

For sample book reviews written by professionals, see the *New York Times Book Review:* http://topics.nytimes.com/topics/features/books/bookreviews/index.html.

Wrap-Up

This chapter looks at a few kinds of dance essays: persuasive essays, reading analysis papers, and book reviews. Philosophical persuasive essays investigate a large question that is not easily answered, such as *What makes a dance beautiful?* Editorial persuasive essays offer an opinion on a contemporary issue, such as men in dance or the place of dance in public schools. Reading analysis papers summarize and analyze one or more articles, revealing the author's attitude toward them. Book reviews describe, analyze, and evaluate a book while emphasizing any unique features that it might have.

*an overhead camera projects their image
the live feed of moving dancers
projected vertically on t
The ground seems*

6

Dance Research
Papers

A research paper requires you to gather information and evidence and synthesize it in a personalized way. Although a research paper is not an opinion paper, it is still guided by your judgment, since you must sort through large amounts of material to determine what is relevant to the points you wish to make. A research paper is not merely a collection of what others have said before on a topic; it is a thoughtful shaping of evidence to support your thesis.

A good research paper asks and answers an intriguing question. Here are some examples: *How are these two choreographers similar and different? How did Asian thought and culture affect the work of modern dance choreographers? What is the history of hip-hop dance, and should we consider it a concert dance form? Was George Balanchine influenced by African-based dance forms? If so, how? How did religion influence the development of dance in the early American colonies? What dances do the Native American Iroquois perform today, and are these dances the same as they were 400 years ago? How do gender roles function in the work of contemporary choreographers?*

Selecting a Topic and Creating a Guiding Question

The topic you choose should be compelling enough to hold your interest over the entire time you will be reading and writing about it. You may have a list of suggested topics to start with, but if not, you might use the list later in this chapter as a starting point. Once you have selected a general topic, you need to narrow it by creating a guiding question, just like guiding questions for essays discussed in chapter 5 and mentioned previously in this chapter. This question will shape your research, and the answer to the question will be the heart of your paper. It might be a question that you already have a hunch about, or it might be a question that you really don't have any idea how to answer. Your research is something like the work of a detective, who must find certain clues and facts in order to make a supported claim.

If you have a topic but no idea what your guiding question might be, you should go right to the library or your computer and begin reading up. Find any books or articles on your topic that look interesting, and begin taking notes. If you know very little about the topic, you might start with an encyclopedia entry in order to get an overview. Look for ideas, works, or choreographers who might provide a focus for your guiding question. Also consider your personal experience and how it relates to the topic. For example, if your topic is comparing George Balanchine to Jerome Robbins, it certainly helps if you have seen some of their work.

In general, if you are working on a particular dance form or choreographer, it is helpful to see examples so that you have a mental image of that dance style. There might be DVDs or videos available through your library or dance program that you can borrow. You can also try finding specific works and choreographers on YouTube or dance company Web sites. Although the quality of the image on YouTube is not very good, it at least provides an overall sense of the choreography or dance style. Seeing dances may evoke questions about them; one of these questions could become your guiding question.

If you are still having trouble finding a guiding question after reading and viewing material on your topic, try watching a DVD or appropriate YouTube footage with a friend or classmate, and then discuss it. What was the most interesting thing you noticed, and why? What would you like to know more about, now that you have seen and read about this person, dance genre, dance issue, and so on?

After creating your guiding question, you may need to narrow your topic even further to suit the length of the paper assigned. Choosing a specific time period can be helpful, as can limiting the number of choreographers or dances discussed. For instance, if you chose to write about the influence of Asian thought and culture on modern dance, you would need to select a few specific choreographers to study, and perhaps limit it to a particular period of time as well. If you were to answer the question about the history of hip-hop dance, you might want to focus on a particular decade or highlight the work of a few artists and styles. The length of your paper is the major determining factor in how much information you will be able to include. You will need to strike a balance between an overly broad and an overly narrow focus. In general, it is better to write in depth about a few people, dances, or events rather than very briefly about many.

Suggested Research Topics

Here are some possible topics that could be used for dance research papers. They are sorted into groups: historical, social issues, aesthetic, and dance education and dance science. With your teacher's approval, you might also create your own topic.

Historical

- History of a particular dance form, such as ballet, bharatanatyam, ballroom, hip-hop, flamenco, contact improvisation
- Compare two dancers, choreographers, or companies, such as these:
    - Marie Salle and Marie Camargo
    - Marie Taglioni and Fanny Elssler
    - Marius Petipa and Michel Fokine
    - New York City Ballet and American Ballet Theatre
    - Isadora Duncan and Ruth St. Denis
    - Martha Graham and Doris Humphrey
    - George Balanchine and Jerome Robbins

- Merce Cunningham and Paul Taylor
- Alvin Ailey American Dance Theater and Dance Theatre of Harlem
- Twyla Tharp and Trisha Brown
- Urban Bush Women and Liz Lerman's Dancers of the Third Age
- Jack Cole and Matt Mattox
- Gregory Hines and Savion Glover

You may create your own pairs for comparison, but make sure that they share some significant traits (such as time period, type of dance, gender, race, philosophical approach, artistic background, or location) in order to make the comparison meaningful. If you select two people or companies who are too dissimilar (such as 18th-century ballerina Marie Camargo and 21st-century choreographer Liz Lerman), there is such a large a gap between them that you would spend all your time pointing out obvious differences.

Social Issues

- Role of race in dance
- Role of gender in dance
- Role of physical ability in dance
- Role of men in dance
- Political commentary in choreography
- Religion, dance, and the American colonies
- Body image in dance
- Sexuality in dance

Aesthetic

- Link between dance and another art form
- Comparison of two dance forms or styles
- Link between Asian art and culture and modern dance
- African roots of contemporary jazz dance
- Martha Graham's use of Emily Dickinson's work
- George Balanchine and African dance forms
- Examination of a specific masterwork (such as Doris Humphrey's "New Dance," Kurt Jooss' "The Green Table," and Alvin Ailey's *Revelations*)

Dance Education and Dance Science

- Dance in the public schools
- Dance and learning
- Dance curriculum in higher education
- Physics in dance
- Kinesiology and dance
- Care and prevention of injury in dance
- Eating disorders in the dance world

A Note About Topics

You may have noticed that the list of topics does not include lists of famous choreographers or dancers to write about individually. That's because this kind of topic tends to produce a paper with little original analysis, and original analysis is an important feature of outstanding dance research papers. It is fairly easy to find information about an artist and then reframe it in your own words without much analysis other than how to organize the material. When you are comparing two artists, some original analysis is built into the topic. It certainly is possible to write about a single artist in an analytical way, but it takes some thought to develop a guiding question more complex than *What are the most important contributions this person has made to dance?* Here is one example of a good guiding question for a research paper on choreographer Katherine Dunham: *How, specifically, does the choreography of Katherine Dunham draw from the time she spent in Haiti, and what significance did that have for modern dance in the mid-20th century?*

More Examples of Guiding Questions

For every topic, there are many possible guiding questions. Here are two examples each for two different topics.

- Topic: bharatanatyam, a classical dance form of India
  - Guiding question 1: Who were a few key figures in the development and preservation of bharatanatyam? (This question narrows a very large topic to a manageable size.

It requires a general knowledge of the subject and then asks the writer to make a judgment about which people to include, which will be defended. The answer to this guiding question then becomes the basis for the thesis statement.)

- Guiding question 2: What is the significance of religion in bharatanatyam, and has it changed over time?
- Topic: Sexuality in Dance
  - Guiding question 1: How and why do today's choreographers use sexuality onstage? (This requires selecting a few choreographers to discuss, which requires familiarity with their work through viewing or reading.)
  - Guiding question 2: How was sexuality expressed through ballet a hundred years ago, and how was it shaped by the social mores of the time?

Bharatanatyam is the oldest classical dance form in India, featuring mythological stories conveyed through intricate movements and gestures.

© Human Kinetics

Primary, Secondary, and Tertiary Sources

Research materials are traditionally divided into primary, secondary, and tertiary sources. Primary sources are the subject of study and are often written by people whom you are researching; secondary sources are written as a commentary on the primary sources. For example, if you were writing about Martha Graham, primary sources would include her autobiography, published interviews, and DVDs of her choreography. Books or articles that discuss and analyze Graham or her work are secondary sources. The value of using primary sources is that you view your subject of study more directly rather than filtered through the lens of critics or historians. However, it is also important to read what highly regarded scholars have to say about the primary sources and the work of the choreographer.

Tertiary (thirdhand) sources are textbooks and encyclopedias; information in these sources is based mainly on secondary sources. Encyclopedias can be useful as a starting point for gathering information and may also help determine whether a Web site's information is valid. They may be used as a quick reference or for fact checking; however, tertiary sources are not usually detailed enough to provide the depth needed when writing a research paper. Never rely mainly on tertiary sources for your information; it is considered poor scholarship and reflects badly on your research skills.

Appropriate Sources

Books, journals, magazines, and newspapers are all possible sources for research papers. Nothing can replace going in person to a good library and browsing the bookshelves. You might happen upon excellent material that you would never find by using your computer. Of course, the reverse is also true—your library's database system can help you find books and articles that you could never find on the bookshelf. Most libraries have an interlibrary loan system that allows access to other book collections in order to boost the size of their holdings. In addition, many libraries have access to electronic databases that can locate articles online, allowing students to download them for free or for a small fee.

Web sites are another source of information. Because of the lack of regulation and fact checking that are customary for print formats such as books and periodicals, Web sites can be full of erroneous information. It is often difficult to determine the reliability and accuracy of information found on Web sites unless you are an expert in that field. Therefore, it's advisable to restrict use of Web sites to primary-source information (i.e., using the Web site of a dance company that you are studying, rather than a secondary-source Web site written by someone else about that dance company). Another option is to use Web sites as supplementary sources only so that you are assured of having mainly validated information from sources that have been reviewed for accuracy, such as online journals or print sources. Sometimes, the Internet is the only source of information for a very recent event or a new dance company; in that case it might be acceptable as a source. Consult with your teacher in advance if you are uncertain about his or her policy on sources.

Video, DVDs, computer streaming of dance performances, interviews with artists, or commentary or analysis on dance issues can also be used as part of your research. Your own commentary on choreography that you have seen is a wonderful addition to a research paper on a particular choreographer, company, or dance genre. It can provide further evidence of a point that you would like to make, or it can elucidate an idea that might otherwise be quite abstract. If you do not have access to DVDs of the choreographers you are studying, try the Internet for access to clips or whole works.

Note Taking

Writing a research paper usually requires a lot of reading. Unfortunately, we can't just deposit all that information into our brains and then sit back and watch it come out of our fingers, magically transformed into a well-written paper. Instead, we must make an effort to comprehend and remember what we read. That is where notes are so important. Note taking obviously helps you remember what you read and what your sources are, but it is more than a memory aid. Note taking actually assists you in the process of assimilating the vast amount of information you encounter while researching your question.

In addition to jotting down the main ideas of each reading, consider "conversing" with it. Write down questions and concerns that occur to you as you read. Is there something that you don't understand? Is there a new interpretation of an old theme or idea? Is there an idea that you strongly agree with or disagree with? Jot it down. Do you see a connection between this article and the one you read earlier? Make a note of it. Also, realize that not every reading will be pertinent to your research; obviously, you won't want to spend time taking notes on something that is of little use.

While reading an article or chapter, you can take notes on large index cards. Later, you can arrange these cards in a way that forms a rough outline for your paper. Or you might prefer to use a computer or notebook where you can keep all your research together. While reading, avoid highlighting as a strategy. The problem with highlighting as you read is that it is difficult to judge the most important elements of the reading until you have finished it and considered it thoughtfully. It is easy to overuse the highlighter, which results in selecting too much material and yields too little useful information when you come to the end of the article. Also, the act of writing or typing actually helps you absorb what you are reading better than the act of highlighting with a marker. The notes you take should include the following information:

- Author, title, place of publication and publisher, date of the source, and (if an article) volume, issue, and page numbers
- Quotations transcribed accurately, with page numbers identified
- Main ideas in each section
- How or if it relates to your guiding question
- Any questions you have about what you read
- Your observations about how a fact or idea relates to something else you've read
- Your observations about how a fact or idea relates to something you've experienced

Once you finish the reading, look at your notes and write a summary of the article that includes your questions and observations as well as the main ideas. At this point, if the article seems as though it is particularly pertinent to your research question, you might want to select a quotation or two that could support a point that you will make in your paper. Be sure to get the page number for the quotation. If the quote is overly long, you may edit out unnecessary words and indicate their absence by inserting ellipses (three spaced periods) in that spot.

Through summarizing, you are forced to think and synthesize what you have just read, as opposed to copying everything in front of you. This initial process of synthesizing leads to piecing the information together from all your sources to create a coherent whole. The process of summarizing will also help you avoid plagiarism, which is a serious offense.

(See also p. 13 in chapter 2 for more on note taking.)

Proper Source Citations

When writing a research paper, you must be careful to give proper credit to those whose ideas and words you use. One kind of information, known as common knowledge, does not have to be attributed, but original ideas and quotations must be cited properly in order to avoid plagiarism.

Plagiarism

The term *plagiarism* comes from the Latin word *plagiarius*, which means kidnapper. Plagiarism is a theft of written material and is regarded as highly unethical, particularly in the academic world. To avoid plagiarism, you must be extremely careful to give credit where credit is due.

In this day, when it is so easy to buy term papers off the Internet, students are often failed on individual papers or for an entire course for the offense of plagiarism. You probably already understand that this form of plagiarism (buying a paper off the Internet or using one written by a friend) is wrong. Not only is it wrong, but it cheats you of an important part of the learning process. If you don't go through the process of reading, synthesizing information, creating a thesis, and writing your paper, you are not participating in the learning process and have missed part of your education. And if these reasons aren't enough to convince you not to plagiarize, remember that members of the faculty have access to computer software that checks research papers for plagiarism, and you are very likely to be caught.

Although it is clear that copying or buying papers is wrong, you may not be aware that using even small bits of the work of others can also be considered plagiarism. There are two main situations in which credit must be given to others: use of quotations and use of ideas. When you use the words of others (and this can apply to even a single significant word), those words must be enclosed in quotation marks and cited either with a footnote or with an in-text note that indicates the source for the quote, its publication year, and the page number that the quotation appears on in the original source. The cited source must also be included in the paper's reference list. Typically, a quotation of two lines or fewer will remain as a part of the running text; a longer quotation will be set as a separate, indented block quote, and no quotation marks are needed. In a research paper, quotations are used to support your points. Quotations from a choreographer or dance artist who is the subject of your paper can add insight about the way that person thinks and uses language. However, your paper should never be more than about 20 percent quotations.

The second situation in which credit must be given is for ideas. This applies to paraphrased material, summaries, and original ideas that spark something totally new. When you paraphrase, even if your words are totally different from the original source, the thought behind the words remains the same, and you must credit the person who first expressed that thought by citing the source in the text (e.g., Smith 2010) and adding its publication information to the reference list. To paraphrase properly without quotation marks, you must avoid using any of the same expressions that the original author wrote. If you do use any of the author's expressions verbatim, you must put those expressions in quotation marks (longer quotes are formatted as an indented block) with page citations.

Quotation, Summary, and Paraphrase

A quotation uses the exact words of a person other than the author and may be taken from any written or spoken source. A summary boils a paragraph down to one main idea or an entire article to a few sentences. A paraphrase repeats the ideas of the original quotation and is roughly the same length, but it's expressed in different words. The following quotation is the opening paragraph from the introduction of Constance Valis Hill's book *Brotherhood in Rhythm*. This book is about the Nicholas brothers, who were famous tap dancers at their peak in the 1930s and '40s:

> Fayard and Harold Nicholas are one of the most beloved teams in dance history. The Nicholas Brothers' exuberant style of American theatrical dance—a melding of jazz, tap, acrobatics, and black vernacular dance—has dazzled vaudeville, theatre, film and television audiences around the world for more than sixty years. They are most often remembered for the daredevil splits, slides, and flips that were sometimes incorporated into their routines; stuck with the "specialty act" label within otherwise all-white Hollywood films, they were variously labeled "eccentric," "acrobatic," and "flash" dancers. But the Nicholas Brothers were more than a "brilliant swing-era flash act." Their rhythmic brilliance, musicality, eloquent footwork, and full-bodied expressiveness are

~ continued

~ continued

unsurpassed, and their dancing represents the most sophisticated refinement of jazz as a percussive dance form. (Hill 2000, 3) Following is an example of a **summary** of the Hill reference:

Although they are best known for their acrobatic dance stunts, the Nicholas brothers also had other qualities that made them outstanding, including their use of rhythm, footwork, expressiveness, and elegance (Hill 2000).

Following is an example of a **paraphrase** of Hill's writing:

Fayard and Harold Nicholas are well known and admired for their energetic type of dance, which blends jazz, tap, acrobatics, and black popular dance, and has been seen for over sixty years. They are mainly remembered for their acrobatic stunts such as splits, slides, and flips, and were often called "flash" dancers. But they did more than those attention-grabbing moves. They also

The famed Nicholas Brothers perform
a tap dancing "flash act" in 1947.

© George Konig/Keystone Features/Getty Images

had exceptional rhythm, musicality, footwork, and expression of the entire body, which made their dancing an elegant form of jazz (Hill 2000).

Even though the words of both the summary and paraphrase are different from the original, the original source still needs to be cited, since the ideas are taken directly from the source. Although many facts about the Nicholas Brothers are common knowledge (i.e., that they are tap dancers known for acrobatic stunts in the 1930s and '40s), the main idea of the paragraph is original (i.e., "their dancing represents the most sophisticated refinement of jazz as a percussive dance form").

Common Knowledge

If the idea that you incorporate into your paper is common knowledge, then there is no need to cite your source. Common knowledge includes the major facts of history, the standard information in any field, and commonsense observations. For instance, birthdates of choreographers, names of their dance works, and the main elements of their choreographic or technical styles would all be common knowledge. Encyclopedia entries are usually based on common knowledge. Folklore (such as fairy tales) and familiar proverbs (such as "a stitch in time saves nine") are additional examples of information that does not need quotation marks and attributions.

Thesis Development

Your thesis is the main point of your paper and will answer your guiding question. Your thesis "will assert something about the topic, conveying your purpose, your opinion, and your attitude" (Fowler 1986, 25). Again, thinking of your research as a question that you are attempting to answer, you may not find your answer until you have done quite a bit of reading. Typically, a thesis is embedded in the first page of a research paper. Usually, some kind of background information and context are necessary before the thesis statement is introduced. Here is a student's example of a good introductory paragraph that includes a brief background discussion of the topic, a research question, and its answer.

THE INNER STRUGGLES OF A DANCER

Professional dancers face numerous hardships within their short careers. There is constant pressure for dancers to be perfect in every move they make, since people are paying a lot of money to see them dance. This pressure can take a very significant toll on the dancer's body and mind. Often, it seems that dance companies put far too much emphasis on this perfection and it often results in serious harm to their dancers. One such harmful result of all this pressure is the all-pressing eating disorder. Are choreographers far too demanding on their dancers? It seems, in many cases, they are.

This introduction does a good job of laying out the territory that will be covered in the paper, along with the writer's main area of concern and her attitude toward it. Her general topic is eating disorders among dancers, but she has posed an interesting question that narrows her focus to the demands of choreographers. It leaves the reader curious about what kinds of demands she will discuss and how, specifically, they might be linked to eating disorders.

Here is an example of how another thesis might be developed and improved. The student chose to write about choreographer Martha Graham's dance titled *Errand Into the Maze*. His research question was (as noted previously) this: What does this dance look like, how is it structured, what do experts have to say about it, and what is its significance? Here is his first attempt at a thesis statement:

Martha Graham's *Errand Into the Maze* is an example of a dance based on Greek mythology.

This is a start because it defines the subject. However, this is a simple statement of fact that does not require much discussion or persuasion. It also does not tell us anything about the dance or the author's attitude toward it. Here is another attempt:

Martha Graham's emotionally tense *Errand Into the Maze* is a good example of how she used Greek mythology as a subject for her dances.

This is better because it gives a sense of the quality of the dance and also qualifies the word example with "good," which will help the discussion. The problem with this is that it sets the stage for discussion of more than one of her dances, since it leads the reader to think of *Errand Into the Maze* as only one example of a larger point that will be made. Here is a third variation:

> Martha Graham's emotionally tense *Errand Into the Maze* is based on the Greek myth of Theseus and the Minotaur, but it creates a new twist by having a female lead.

This thesis is the best of the three because it gives information both about the dance and about the author's attitude toward it. It mentions the Greek myth on which the dance is based, but it goes beyond that obvious connection to deliver an assertion that also takes into account Graham's interest in pushing boundaries.

Structure

Your writing is held together not only by the meaning of what you are saying but also by the way in which it is structured. The structure of the research paper, as in a persuasive essay, follows the format of introduction, body, and conclusion. The length of the body will vary depending on the length of the paper, but no matter its length, each paragraph in the body will make a point related to the thesis. A paper with a strong, well-supported thesis and a logical conclusion will have coherence and satisfy the reader.

Sample Structure for a Research Paper

The body will have more than two points, but the structure is the same as presented for each.

Title (reflects topic and your analysis)

   I. Introduction
      A. Context and topic
      B. Thesis statement

  II. Body
      A. Point 1
         1. Example
         2. Example
         3. Example
      B. Point 2
         1. Example
         2. Example
         3. Example

 III. Conclusion

Writing Process

How do you go about converting all of this organized information into an intelligent research paper? In the process of taking notes, you will probably have become quite familiar with the subject. Your job is to explain and analyze your subject in a way that will engage and educate your reader. A good way to begin this stage of your paper is to organize your notes.

Organizing Your Notes

Once you have completed your note taking, organize your notes in a logical way, which might be by choreographer, by dance work, by dance company, chronologically, or by some other method that suits your needs. Each of the sources you used will fit into the outline (presented previously) in one or more places. If you used index cards for your notes, you can actually lay the cards in various orders to see what works best (Hudson 2006, 33). You can see approximately how many points you will be able to make, given the length of your paper, and what kinds of examples to use for each. When you begin writing, you will link each of these points together, remembering that everything needs to be related to your thesis.

To Free-Write or Not?

Is it possible to free-write when you are working on a research paper? Free writing, as described in chapter 2, page 16, is used for developing your own thoughts (in the case of a persuasive essay) or your own impressions of a dance performance (in the case of a critique) or a book (in the case of a book review). It is not so easy to free-write when you must keep in mind the ideas and opinions of experts other than you. However, it is possible to do a variation on free writing that can be useful in the beginning stages of shaping your research paper.

Once you have determined the thesis of your paper, you may use that as the basis for a free write. Type or write the thesis at the top of your paper, and then write freely about it, without looking at your references, for about 20 minutes. Write using whatever information you can recall from your reading and note taking, but don't worry if you can't remember a source. Also include your own analysis and interpretation of the information. Your main goal is to create a flow of ideas. Once you have finished your free write, look it over and fill in source information. Integrate the free write with your overall organization of ideas.

Putting It All Together

Once you know your thesis and have an idea of which points you will use to support it, you simply need to sit down and write. Starting with your introduction, give the reader a context for your topic—some background information that will set the stage for your thesis statement. Your introduction will probably be one paragraph long, with the thesis sentence near the end of the paragraph, but other configurations are possible. For a longer paper, your introduction may be two or three paragraphs.

After you've finished your introduction, move on to the body of your paper. Keeping your notes by your side, write out each point or paragraph, making sure to develop it adequately. Begin each paragraph with a topic sentence that tells the reader what you will discuss, and then offer details and analysis of that topic throughout the paragraph. Examples of the points you are making are essential; use quotations sparingly to support your points.

Finally, wrap up your paper with a strong conclusion, which summarizes your main ideas using a fresh perspective. Make sure that your conclusion and your thesis match up; it is easy to wander off the track onto an interesting subtopic when you write and then forget to come back to your original intention.

Flow

After your writing is complete, you will need to make sure that it has good flow. Logical writing flows easily from thought to thought, like a car moving smoothly ahead. When a driver encounters an old fender in the road, she is forced to stop or swerve to avoid it. The flow of the car trip has been interrupted, and the driver must take a moment to comprehend what happened before resuming the journey. Similarly, a reader faced with a gap in logic is forced to stop or swerve while reading. In your paper, each idea should lead clearly to the next, allowing the reader to experience a smooth ride. The paragraphs of the sample paper at the end of this chapter have good flow.

Equally as important as flow within a paragraph is flow among paragraphs. Each paragraph needs to transition smoothly to the next, unless you are dividing your text with subheadings. Subheadings are not recommended for shorter papers (under 10 pages), so unless your paper is quite long, keep your thoughts connected between paragraphs.

Writing Style

Even the most interesting topic will not engage the reader if it contains grammatical errors. Good grammar, accurate spelling, and a clear writing style are very important to the success of your paper; your content can be communicated only through good form. Any technical errors reduce the effectiveness of your writing, even if you have good ideas and a strong thesis.

Some common writing concerns (audience, punctuation, syntax, compound and complex sentences, spell check, and gender-inclusive language) are discussed in chapter 2 beginning on page 19.

Editorial Style

Editorial style is a consistent way of handling all the details of writing that mainly affect how it looks rather than what it says. Editorial style covers punctuation, abbreviations, charts and tables, citations of references, and many other fine points. There are many of these styles, which have evolved over the past century or more. Each style was created to serve the needs of a particular publishing organization; for example, the Chicago style was created by the University of Chicago Press shortly after its founding in 1891 when they needed to establish consistency among the proofreaders whose job involved correcting errors. The first version of the *Chicago Manual of Style* (CMS) was published in 1906 (www.chicagomanualofstyle. org/about15_history.html).

Two other well-known editorial styles are Modern Language Association (MLA) and American Psychological Association (APA). The MLA style is used predominantly for writing on language and literature and is used internationally as well as in the United States. The APA style is used mostly in the fields of social science, business, economics, nursing, social work, and physical education. All three styles have been used at various times by dance scholars, depending on what is required by their publishers. This book uses the CMS author–date system, which offers brief in-text citations that make it easy to see who is quoted. An Internet guide to CMS is at www.chicagomanualofstyle.org, and a hard copy should be available in the reference section of your library. Be aware that Web addresses change; you may need to do a search for the latest version of a style manual online.

Following are examples of references and in-text citations for the three styles mentioned previously: CMS, MLA, and APA. You will see sample entries for books, journals, online journals, newspapers, DVDs, and Internet sites. Since all three editorial styles are used by dance writers, you may use whichever one your instructor prefers. For all styles, be sure to italicize the names of books, journals, magazines, newspapers, and DVDs. For more detailed information, consult either the online or hard-copy versions of these style guides.

Chicago Author–Date Style

The two main components of the CMS author–date style are a reference list at the end of the paper, which includes a full list of all works mentioned, and short in-text citations in parentheses. The citations are inserted in the paper in parentheses wherever there is a mention of an author, a source, or an author's idea and also after any quotation.

Following are some examples of entries for citations in the text and in the reference section. The reference list for this book can also serve as a model for CMS style. Title your reference page "References" and list all sources alphabetically by the surname of the author. If no author is given, then use the title of the article or book. Note that only the first word of article titles is capitalized in the reference list, along with the first word after a colon, and there are no quotation marks around article titles. Page numbers are not included in in-text citations unless you are quoting.

Book

- A book citation in text contains just the author's surname, the date of publication, and the page (if you are quoting a specific place in the book): (Bean 1996, 5). Note that there is no comma between name and date, but there is one between the date and page number.
- A book listed in the references looks like this: Bean, J. 1996. *Engaging ideas: The professor's guide to integrating writing, critical thinking, and active learning in the classroom.* San Francisco: Jossey-Bass.

- Book with two authors in text citation: (Gottschalk and Hjortshoj 2004).

- Book with two authors in references: Gottschalk, K., and K. Hjortshoj. 2004. *The elements of teaching writing: A resource for instructors in all disciplines.* Boston: Bedford/St. Martin's Press.

- Article in an edited book in text citation: (Jowitt 2001, 7-11).

- Article in an edited book in references: Jowitt, D. 2001. Beyond description: Writing beneath the surface. In *Moving history, dancing cultures*, edited by A. Dils and A.C. Albright. Middletown, CT: Wesleyan Press, 7-11.

Journal

- Journal article in text citation: (Emig 1997, 122-28).

- Journal article in references: Emig, J. 1997. Writing as a mode of learning. *College Composition and Communication* 28: 122-28.

Online Journal

- Online journal in text citation: (Carter et al. 2007).

- Online journal in references: Carter, M., Ferzli, M., and Wiebe, E. 2007. Writing to learn by learning to write in the disciplines. *Journal of Business and Technical Communication* 21, no. 3 (July), http://jbt.sagepub.com/cgi/reprint/21/3/278. You do not need to include the date that the journal was accessed.

Newspaper

- Newspaper review in text citation: (Kisselgoff 1991, C3).

- Newspaper review in references: Kisselgoff, A. 1991. A *Giselle* celebration, from pure to romantic. Review. *New York Times*, June 7.

Web Page

- Web page in text citation: (NDEO 2005).

- Web page in references: National Dance Education Organization. 2005. *Standards for learning and teaching dance in the arts: Ages 5-18.* www.ndeo.org/standards.asp.

DVD

- DVD, video, or film in text citation: (Graham 1984).

- DVD, video, or film in references: Graham, M. 1984. VHS. *Three contemporary classics.* New York: Video Artists International.

Modern Language Association (MLA)

MLA uses brief in-text citations similar to those in CMA style but without dates. They include the author's surname followed by the relevant page numbers. At the end of your paper, the reference list is titled "Works Cited" and arranged alphabetically by author's surname or by title if a name is not available. Note that article titles are in quotation marks and are capitalized in the same way as book titles. The sample research paper in this chapter uses MLA editorial style.

Book

A reference to an entire book is best done by mentioning the author and book title in the text without parentheses.

- A reference to an idea or quotation from the book is cited in parentheses: (Bean 5). Note that there is no comma between the name and the page number.

- A book listed in works cited looks like this: Bean, John. *Engaging Ideas: The Professor's Guide to Integrating Writing, Critical Thinking, and Active Learning in the Classroom.* San Francisco: Jossey-Bass, 1996.

- Book with two authors in text citation: (Gottschalk and Hjortshoj 151).

- Book with two authors in works cited: Gottschalk, Karen, and Keith Hjortshoj. *The Elements of Teaching Writing: A Resource for Instructors in All Disciplines.* Boston: Bedford/St. Martin's Press, 2004.

- Article in an edited book in text citation: (Jowitt 7-11).

- Article in an edited book in works cited: Jowitt, Deborah. "Beyond Description: Writing Beneath the Surface." In *Moving History, Dancing Cultures,* eds. Ann Dils and Ann Cooper Albright. Middletown: Wesleyan Press, 2001.

Journal

- Journal article in text citation: (Emig 122).

- Journal article in works cited: Emig, Janet. "Writing as a Mode of Learning." *College Composition and Communication* 28 (1997): 122-128.

Online Journal

- Online journal in text citation: (Carter et al. 278-302).

- Online journal in works cited: Carter, Michael, Miriam Ferzli, and Eric Wiebe. "Writing to Learn by Learning to Write in the Disciplines." *Journal of Business and Technical Communication* 21.3 (2007): 278-302. 1 May, 2009 <http://jbt.sagepub.com/cgi/reprint/21/3/278>.

Newspaper

- Newspaper review in text citation: (Kisselgoff C3)
- Newspaper review in works cited: Kisselgoff, Anna. "A *Giselle* Celebration, from Pure to Romantic." Review. *New York Times* 7 June 1991: C3.

Web Page (Including Image Sites Such as YouTube)

Since many Web pages are not numbered, include the paragraph number as a reference point if quoting. Also, many Web pages do not list a particular author, so the title of the article should be used as the author's name.

- Web page in text citation: ("About Dance Education" par. 3).
- Web page in works cited: "About Dance Education in the United States." National Dance Education Organization. 23 May 2009. <www.ndeo.org/content.aspx?page_id=22&club_id=893257&module_id=56441>.

DVD, Video, or Film

- In text citation: (*Three Contemporary Classics*, VHS).
- In works cited: *Three Contemporary Classics*. Chor. Martha Graham. 1984. VHS. New York: Artists International.

American Psychological Association (APA)

APA style uses an author–date style of in-text citations that is slightly different from the CMS version. APA uses a reference page at the end of the paper titled "References." Only the first word of article or book titles is capitalized, along with the first word after the colon.

Book

- Citation in text: (Bean, 1996, p. 5). The page number is needed only if you are quoting material.
- In reference list: Bean, J. (1996). *Engaging ideas: The professor's guide to integrating writing, critical thinking, and active learning in the classroom.* San Francisco: Jossey-Bass.

- Book with two authors in text citation: (Gottschalk & Hjortshoj, 2004, p. 151)
- In reference list: Gottschalk, K. & Hjorshoj, K. (2004). *The elements of teaching writing: A resource for instructors in all disciplines.* Boston: Bedford/St. Martin's Press.
- Article in an edited book in text citation: (Jowitt, 2001, p. 7). The page number is needed only if you are quoting.
- Article in an edited book in reference list: Jowitt, D. (2001). Beyond description: Writing beneath the surface. In A. Dils & A.C. Albright (Eds.), *Moving history, dancing cultures* (pp. 7-11). Middletown, CT: Wesleyan Press.

Journal

- Journal article in text citation: (Emig, 1997, p. 122)
- Journal article in references: Emig, J. (1997). Writing as a mode of learning. *College composition and communication 28*(2), 122-128.

Online Journal

- Online journal in text citation: (Carter et al., 2007).
- Online journal in reference list: Carter, M., Ferzli, M., & Wiebe, E. (2007). Writing to learn by learning to write in the disciplines. *Journal of Business and Technical Communication, 21*(3), 278-302. http://jbt.sagepub.com/cgi/reprint/21/3/278. Retrieved May 1, 2009.

Newspaper

- Newspaper review in text citation: (Kisselgoff, 1991, C3).
- Newspaper review in references: Kisselgoff, A. (1991, June 7). A *Giselle* celebration, from pure to romantic. [Review of *Giselle*]. *New York Times*, C3.

Web Page

- Web page in text citation: ("About Dance Education," 2005).
- Web page in references: About dance education in the United States. (2005). National Dance Education Organization. www.ndeo.org/content.aspx?page_id=22&club_id=893257&module_id=56441. Retrieved May 23, 2009.

Rubric for Dance Research Papers

A rubric is a set of criteria indicating how an assignment will be evaluated, usually giving specific qualities of papers at the levels of excellent, good, adequate, and poor, although the number of levels may vary. The rubrics in this book use four levels. Rubrics are useful because when you know the specific criteria by which papers are graded, you are more likely to do a good job with the assignment. There are seven elements in the rubric for research papers (see table 6.1), which are explained here:

1. *Introduction* includes a context for the topic and an interesting assertion.
2. *Thesis statement* indicates topic and author's attitude toward it, with an original insight.
3. *Ideas and development* include supporting details, appropriate research, synthesis of information, and a unique perspective on topic.
4. Paper *flows* smoothly and logically while maintaining reader interest.
5. *Conclusion* ties the paper together.
6. *Conventions of English language* are followed accurately.
7. *References* are appropriate, reputable, and adequate in number; *documentation* includes proper use of citations and format.

Sample From Dance Research Paper

Following is a student's research paper about the ways in which two choreographers, Jerome Robbins and Bob Fosse, approach dance in musical theater. The title encapsulates a major point that the author will make and names the choreographers who will be examined. The introductory paragraph gives background on the topic, and the thesis of the paper is two sentences near the end of the paragraph:

> While Robbins and Fosse agreed on the significance of and potential for dance in musical theatre, they differed in their approach. Robbins sought to mold his dances to the characters and story, whereas Fosse created a trademark style and imposed it on each musical project.

Discussion of these two ideas constitutes the substance of the paper.

Some strong points of the paper include its well-written, unified paragraphs; examples to support its points; and good use of supporting quotations. The author cites ideas that come from other sources, even when they are stated in her own words. The conclusion repeats the main points of the paper, but with a new twist: it links Robbins to the idea of immersion, and Fosse to alienation. In addition to using good grammar, spelling, and punctuation, the paper has excellent flow because each thought leads smoothly to the next. This paper uses the MLA editorial style.

DANCING AS STORYTELLING:
THE INNOVATIONS OF ROBBINS AND FOSSE

Elena Blyskal, Providence College

No discussion of twentieth-century musical theater can be complete without acknowledging—and celebrating—the contributions of Jerome Robbins and Bob Fosse. Both Robbins and Fosse greatly enhanced the role of dance in musical theater. Each of their choreography is just as integral to the plot as music and dialogue, an achievement that was not previously experienced with dance. While Robbins and Fosse agreed on the significance of and potential for dance in musical theater, they greatly differed in their approach. Robbins sought to mold his dances to the characters and story, whereas Fosse created a trademark style and imposed it on each musical project. Despite their differences, both Robbins' and Fosse's influence on the development of dance in musical theater cannot be denied— and the musicals of today certainly could not exist without it.

The development of dance in musical theater did not begin with Robbins or Fosse. That achievement belongs to Agnes de Mille, who revolutionized musical theater in 1943 with her choreography of *Oklahoma!* (Dalinsky). Her vision of Laurey's dream ballet opened the door for dance's contribution to plot and character development. This function had previously belonged only to music, lyrics and dialogue; dancing in musical theater was usually mere entertainment that was unrelated to the action. While this accomplishment did make great strides for dance, "this scene [the dream ballet] is set apart from the environment the characters live in, and stand-in dancers perform their roles" (Dalinsky par. 1). Therefore, Robbins took

Table 6.1   Rubric for Research Paper

Expectation	Level 4	Level 3	Level 2	Level 1
Introduction	Gives context, identifies topic, and makes an interesting assertion.	Gives context, identifies topic, and makes an assertion.	Gives little or no context, and identifies topic without a clear assertion.	Lacks clear beginning altogether.
Thesis statement	Gives good indication of topic, offers an original insight, and indicates writer's attitude.	Gives good indication of topic and writer's attitude.	Gives some indication of topic or writer's attitude.	Lacks thesis, or thesis gives little indication of topic or writer's attitude.
Ideas and development	Supporting details are accurate, relevant, and helpful; uses appropriate research; evidence of synthesis; illuminates topic in unique way.	Supporting details are accurate, relevant, and helpful; uses appropriate research; evidence of synthesis.	Supporting details are somewhat accurate, relevant, and helpful; uses some appropriate research; some evidence of synthesis.	Lacks supporting details or accuracy; uses little appropriate research; little evidence of synthesis.
Flow	Each paragraph relates to its topic sentence; thoughts flow logically; transitions between paragraphs are smooth; syntax is varied and language is interesting.	Each paragraph relates to its topic sentence; thoughts usually flow logically; transitions between paragraphs are often smooth; syntax is varied.	Each paragraph usually relates to its topic sentence; thoughts sometimes flow logically; syntax is sometimes repetitive or confusing.	Paragraphs are disorganized and illogical; syntax is problematic.
Conclusion	Summarizes writer's observations in an interesting way; adds new insight.	Summarizes writer's observations and may also add new insight.	Partially summarizes writer's observations.	Lacks clarity or no conclusion offered.
Conventions of English language	0-2 errors in spelling, punctuation, and grammar.	3-5 errors in spelling, punctuation, and grammar.	6-8 errors in spelling, punctuation, and grammar.	More than 8 errors in spelling, punctuation, and grammar.

Expectation	Level 4	Level 3	Level 2	Level 1
References and documentation	Uses more than adequate number of varied and reputable resources; uses proper format (i.e., CMS, APA, or MLA style); gives credit for all quotations; cites sources for ideas (other than author's) that are not common knowledge.	Uses adequate number of varied and reputable sources; uses mostly proper format (i.e., CMS, APA, or MLA style); gives credit for all quotations and most ideas (other than author's) that are not common knowledge.	Uses either too few resources or some that are not appropriate; problems with proper format; gives credit for some quotations or ideas that are not common knowledge.	References are inadequate; improper documentation format; lacks credit for quotations and ideas that are not common knowledge.

de Mille's idea and ran with it—the performers in his musicals would sing, dance, *and* act. In addition, the choreography would contribute just as much to the plot development as music and dialogue; dance's involvement in the story would be equal and consequential, not occasional.

Examples of dance's significance and prevalence in Robbins' musical are countless. For instance, *Fiddler on the Roof*'s "Tevye's Dream" serves as both a spectacular production number and a major pivot point in the plot. The ensemble brings Tevye's fabricated nightmare to life through a combination of dream-like, comic and horrific movement and dance. However, this sequence is not only entertaining but also required in order for the action to proceed; character choices are made and key information is revealed that enable the following events to occur. In *Gypsy*, June's vaudeville acts serve as milestones that indicate different locales and the passage of time. However, perhaps no example is more timeless than *West Side Story* when entire scenes are unfolded with need for only movement and music, not text. Indeed, dance was no longer just diversion. It had evolved past dance in its isolated self—what the audience was watching was always the story, simply told through a different medium. Robbins defended this vision as he discussed his collaboration with the other two *West Side Story* creators:

Why did we have to do it separately and elsewhere? Why did Lenny [Bernstein] have to write an opera, Arthur [Laurents] a play, me a ballet? Why couldn't we, in aspiration, try to bring our deepest talents together . . .? That was the true *gesture* of the show. (Jowitt 266)

Although Robbins exploded on the musical theater scene before Fosse, Fosse strove toward a similar goal with his choreography, also experiencing great success. Similarly to Robbins' shows, Fosse's projects as both choreographer and director—including *Damn Yankees, Sweet Charity, Pippin* and *Chicago*—elevated the function of dance to a more prominent level for storytelling. Gary Kilmer, a swing in Broadway's *Chicago*, explains that Fosse "didn't believe in dance for dance's sake . . .

West Side Story choreographed by Jerome Robbins, 1980 Broadway revival starring Debbie Allen.

Billy Rose Theatre Division, The New York Public Library for the Performing Arts, Astor, Lenox and Tilden Foundations.

dances weren't a pause in the action. They were a continuation of the story" (Mettler par. 13). Some of the most pivotal plot points in Fosse's musicals were told through dance, whether it was feeding the press a fabricated story ("We Both Reached for the Gun," *Chicago)* or introducing a curious young man to sex ("With You/The Flesh," *Pippin*).

Along with propelling the plot, both Robbins and Fosse were renowned for prioritizing acting and emotion in their choreography. Robbins himself had intensively studied acting, training in the "Method" at the Actors Studio by Elia Kazan. To enhance the credibility of the performances and the depth of character development, Robbins would often go to extremes during the rehearsal process. During *West Side Story*, he "expected the cast to live their parts, using only their characters' names during rehearsal and sitting with their fellow gang members for lunch" (Dalinsky par. 14). However, Fosse upheld similar standards, insisting, "You can't be a good dancer unless you're a good actor. Otherwise it's all just so much animated wallpaper!" (Beddow par. 3). An occasional actor as well, he infused every step with underlying meaning and emotion. This goal is most evident in Fosse's style itself—famous for its subtle body-part isolations rather than large, sweeping gestures. "By isolating specific movements, Fosse helps communicate emotion, plot and character. . . . The isolation clearly tells the audience where to look and how to feel" (Partridge par. 2).

It is with the exploration of style that the similarities between Fosse and Robbins end. While these two choreographer-directors maintained similar insights into dance's function within a musical, their actual choreographic approaches were altogether different. Robbins' ballet training contrasted with Fosse's jazz and vaudeville background is by no means the only divergence. Although Robbins was largely influenced by ballet his whole life, classical ballet still prioritized sweeping, "direct presentation of movement" over dramatic individual characterizations (Teachout par. 10). Stemming perhaps from his training as an actor, Robbins sought to realistically reflect the characters of the play within his choreography. For instance, he expanded his ballet vocabulary so that the cast of *West Side Story* would move more honestly as street kids (Dalinsky par. 12). As Robbins once asserted:

The possibilities of the human body are endless. Why not use them all? Why limit ourselves to a set language which, in spite of its good qualities, is no longer fit to express the feelings and problems of today? (Dalinsky 19)

Therefore, it is difficult to attribute one singular style to Robbins, because his dances ranged from the strut of a trumpet-toting stripper to the reverent folk dances of a Jewish village in Russia. Rather than invent an entirely new style, he often infused existing dance styles with his own ideas based on the circumstances of the play. For instance, *West Side Story*'s "Dance at the Gym" utilizes the popular dances of mambo and cha-cha for a higher purpose. As the choreography pulsates with "sexual, territorial energy" (Jacobs par. 6), the Sharks and Jets use these styles as means for competition, as outlets for expressing their hostility and frustration. In *Fiddler on the Roof* he uses ritualistic elements that he observed himself at Jewish weddings (Jowitt 353). Robbins was comfortable in whatever idiom was necessary.

Fosse worked from an individually based perspective as well, albeit producing an altogether different result. He approached his choreography through the dancer's point of view, not necessarily the character's. Using individual dancers' physical idiosyncrasies, he created a unique style that he then imposed on many different stories; while Robbins worked from the inside out, Fosse worked from the outside in. Indeed, Fosse's style was largely autobiographical, considering both his capabilities as a dancer and the effects of his life experiences on his work. His unique choreography originated from his own physical traits—rather than hide his quirks, he fused them into a fresh, innovative movement vocabulary. "The hunched-over back came from Fosse's poor posture; the knock-kneed, turned-in stances came from his lack of turnout; and the trademark black bowler hat was a way of hiding his balding head" (Partridge par. 4).

However, this style was not only performed by Fosse alone. Fosse was known for acknowledging his dancers' varied body types and tailoring his movement to fit the person's shape (Mettler par. 9). His dancers were showcased as individuals.

Although Fosse may have considered his dancers more than their characters while choreographing, there is no doubt that the specificity of his movements—not to mention the subtlety of a shoulder roll, an eyebrow lift, a single unexpected kick— aided tremendously in communicating character.

While Robbins was attracted to vastly different projects, adopting an appropriate dance vocabulary for each new situation, Fosse was drawn to plays of similar content to which he could apply his own style. Motifs of sexuality, corruption, decadence, and cynicism appear throughout his works (e.g., *Chicago, Pippin, Cabaret*, and *Sweet Charity*), which further testifies to Fosse's tendency toward the autobiographical. We rarely know Robbins' personal point of view from his choreography, yet Fosse's is unmistakable. As an amateur child vaudevillian, Fosse grew up performing in seedy strip clubs; his shows also feature low-life types and themes of depression, indulgence and futility (Acocella 325). Robbins takes us from the gang streets of New York to pre-World War I Russia, but the story that Fosse tells is the same story over and over again—his story.

Immersion is to Robbins what alienation is to Fosse. Robbins disappeared into the musical in every sense, creating whatever dance would honestly bring that world to life. Meanwhile, Fosse removed his audience just enough to give them a harsh dose of reality, an alienating reality that is conveyed through his consistently cold, isolated movements. However, both Robbins and Fosse—in ways not surpassed since—have ingeniously mastered the ultimate goal of the theatrical performing artist: the art of storytelling.

Works Cited

Acocella, Joan. *Twenty-Eight Artists and Two Saints.* New York: Random House, 2007.

Beddow, Margery. "Working with Bob Fosse." *Dance Spirit* 7 (Jul./Aug. 2003): 65. 30 March 2008. <http://search.ebscohost.com>.

Dalinsky, Maya. "The Dance Master: The Legacy of Jerome Robbins." *Humanities* 25.5 (Sept./Oct. 2004): 22-25. 30 March 2008. <http://search.ebscohost.com>.

Jacobs, Laura. "Jerome Robbins, 1918-1998." *New Criterion* 17 (Sept. 1998): 48-50. 30 March 2008. <www.newcriterion.com/articles.cfm/robbins-jacobs-3015>.

Jowitt, Deborah. *Jerome Robbins: His Life, His Theatre, His Dance*. New York: Simon & Schuster, 2004.

Mettler, Lyn. "The Fosse Phenomenon." *Dance Spirit* 7 (1 July 2003): 62-65. 30 March 2008. <http://search.ebscohost.com>.

Partridge, Jewel Elizabeth. "Fosse Footnotes." *Dance Spirit* 8 (Jan. 2004): 68. 30 March 2008. <http://search.ebscohost.com>.

Teachout, Terry. "Choreography by Jerome Robbins." *Commentary* 103 (Apr. 1997): 58-62. 30 March 2008. <http://search.ebscohost.com>.

Wrap-Up

Dance research papers ask and answer an intriguing guiding question. Topics for research can focus on history, issues in the art, aesthetics, or specific branches of research such as dance medicine or dance education. After reading widely on your topic, you will need to narrow your focus, such as by selecting a specific period or a few choreographers to examine in depth. As you take notes for your paper, write down the main ideas in each article or chapter, and "converse" by also jotting down questions and observations about the material. Don't forget to copy a few appropriate quotations with complete source information, including page numbers. Sources for your paper can be primary, secondary, or tertiary and must be cited properly to avoid plagiarism. Your writing style should be logical, informative, and interesting; your editorial style should be consistent throughout, according to the guidelines of *Chicago Manual of Style* (University of Chicago Press 2003), *MLA Style Manual and Guide to Scholarly Publishing* (Gibaldi 1998), or *Publication Manual of the American Psychological Association* (2009).

appendix

Observation and Discussion Exercise for Critiquing Dance

Class: Any class where students need to practice critiquing dance.

Objectives: To give students practice in describing, analyzing, interpreting, and evaluating theatrical dance works; to encourage exchange of ideas among students; to develop students' aesthetic sense.

Overview: An in-class exercise that takes 1 to 2 hours. First, a video view of a dance work, approximately 10 to 20 minutes in length, followed by a structured discussion in small groups or as a class.

Conversation about dances is a good prelude to writing about them. Discussion will highlight the notion that there is no one correct way to see a dance; different viewers will be more or less attuned to different aspects of a piece, and sharing those differences will help make the total vision of a dance more complete.

The Feldman model (see p. 69 in chapter 4) suggests an approach to discussing the arts that includes description, analysis, interpretation, and evaluation, in that order. Following are questions that pertain to each that can be used as the basis for discussion. Once students have had practice using these questions, future discussions may be more open ended.

Description

In this exercise, description involves a simple inventory of movement and supporting elements: space, time, weight, flow, level, shape, dynamics, pedestrian movement, gesture, physical contact, focus, music, sound, text, lighting, costumes, environment, set, and props.

Questions About Movements

The most important element in dance is movement, which can be analyzed and discussed in detail.

- Space is the area in which the dance is performed and the directions, levels, pathways, shapes, and designs created by bodies moving through space.
  - How does the choreographer use space in the dance?
  - Do dancers move primarily in straight or in curved pathways?
  - Is there a particular section of the dance that emphasizes straight or curved pathways?
  - Do the dancers cover a lot of space, or do they stay in one spot?
  - Are spatial patterns important in the dance? If so, which ones?
- Level in dance refers to how close or far from the floor the dancers are.
  - Are the dancers upright (high level), crouched or kneeling (middle level), or on the floor (low level)?
  - Are high levels accentuated through the use of aerial movements or partnering?
- Shape refers to the formations made by bodies during the dance.
  - What kinds of shapes do you notice?
  - Are they created by individual dancers, by pairs, or by groups of dancers?
  - Are they symmetrical or asymmetrical?
  - Does the choreographer deemphasize shape by stressing constant flow of movement?
- Time in dance refers to duration, tempo, and rhythm.
  - How does the choreographer use time in the dance?
  - What is the tempo (speed) of the dance? Does it change tempos?
  - Are all the dancers moving at the same speed?
  - What is its duration (length)?
  - What kinds of rhythms are used? (A rhythm is a pattern of beats.)

- Is the movement primarily detached, or is it sustained? (Detached movement has a stop-and-start quality, whereas sustained movement is continuous.)
- Dynamics refer to movement quality, which is how the movement is performed rather than what the movement is.
  - Is the movement quality large or small, fast or slow, tense or relaxed, smooth or choppy?
  - What other movement qualities do you see?
  - Can you name two or three qualities that predominate in one section of the dance?
- Weight refers to the quality of weight in the body, not how much the dancers weigh!
  - Do the dancers seem to pull away from gravity in an upward direction, or do they give in to gravity in a downward direction?
  - Does the movement seem heavy or light?
  - Is the movement done with a strong or a light force?
- Pedestrian movement is everyday movement, which comes from ordinary life activities, such as walking, running, sitting, and performing simple tasks. Is there pedestrian movement in this dance?
- Gesture is a movement of a specific part of the body, such as the head, hand, or arm; it has a commonly understood meaning. Some examples are shrugging the shoulders, shaking the head, and pointing a finger. Are there body gestures in this dance? If so, which ones?
- Physical contact involves dancers touching one another.
  - Is there physical contact between or among the dancers?
  - What kind of contact is it?
- Eye focus and facial expression refer to how dancers use their faces to convey meaning.
  - Where do the dancers look?
  - Do the dancers tend to look more at the audience, at each other, or somewhere else?
  - How do the dancers use their faces?
  - Are they clearly expressing emotions as they dance, or are their faces generally neutral?

Questions About Supporting Elements
The accompaniment for a dance can have a strong influence on the audience's perception of a performance.

- Music, sound, or text
  - What is the accompaniment for this dance?
  - If there is music, who is the composer?
  - What instruments or voices are used?
  - What kind of music is it?
  - Is it live or recorded?
  - If the accompaniment is sounds, what are they?
  - If there is text, who wrote it, and what does it say?
- Costumes
  - What are the color, fit, and style of the costumes?
  - Did all of the dancers wear the same costumes?
- Lighting
  - Was the lighting generally dark or bright?
  - What colors did you notice?
  - How did the lighting change during the dance?
  - Was there anything special that you noticed about the lighting?
- Performance environment
  - Where is this dance concert performed?
    - Proscenium theater is most commonly used for dance concerts. All the dancing takes place onstage behind a large proscenium arch, usually delineated by curtains.
    - Thrust stage juts out into the house (theater), generally surrounded on three sides by audience. No curtains are used to separate the audience and performers.
    - Open performance space, such as a gymnasium or dance studio, may be arranged in any fashion. Seating may face one direction only or may totally surround the performers.
    - Alternative performing environment is any space that is not usually used for performance, including parks, zoos, art museums, and lobbies. Environmental dance is a piece that has been designed specifically for a particular non-performance location, such as outdoors next to a lake.

- Did you notice anything interesting or unusual about the performance space?
- Set is everything fixed that is in the performing area and may include a backdrop, furniture, sculpture, a building, and other objects. Was there a stage set for the performance? If so, what did it look like?
- Stage properties, or props, are moveable objects, usually small enough to be manipulated by the performers. Are any props used, such as a ball, scarf, or chair? If so, what are they and what adjectives might describe them?

Analysis

Analysis builds on description and suggests comparing, contrasting, and studying interrelationships, structure, and style. These questions prompt you to consider the structure and style of the dance.

Questions to Consider for Analysis

- Sections
  - Are there sections in the dance? How many?
  - How could you tell one section from the next?
  - Could you tell the difference between the beginning, middle, and end?
  - What kinds of contrasts did you see among the sections?
- Relationship of movement to music: Did the structure of the dance mimic that of the music? If so, how?
- Development
  - Did the dance change over time?
  - What was the development like?
  - Was there a climax (high point) in the dance? If so, what was it? If not, why not?
- Theme and variation: Does the choreographer repeat a movement idea throughout the piece? If so, describe it.
- Canon: Does the choreographer use a canon, or round (like "Row, Row, Row Your Boat") structure anywhere in the dance?
- Preferred movements: What kinds of movements are used the most?
- Style: How would you describe the style of this dance?

Interpretation

When interpreting a dance, you are making meaning from it as it relates to you personally but also on a broader level. All dances are made within a particular sociocultural context and relate to the traditions and values of that time and place. Knowing and understanding the varied kinds of human movement and expression that are typical of the cultural group making a particular dance are important in interpreting it.

Questions to Consider for Interpretation

- Title: Does the title give any insight into the meaning of the dance? If so, how?
- Program notes: Was there any information in the program that is useful in interpretation? If so, what is it?
- Content: Did this dance have a narrative, message, mood, or theme that you could identify? (Even abstract dances have one or more organizing ideas.)
- Cultural context: Are you familiar with the cultural context in which the dance was created? If so, how might that help you interpret the work? If not, can you find any information in your library or online that would help you?
- Choreographer: Do you know anything about the choreographer that might be useful in interpreting this dance?
- Personal meaning
  - Were there any connections between what you saw in the performance and your own life experience?
  - Were there specific movements that reminded you of something?

Evaluation

Evaluation is the judging of the merit or success of a dance based on several factors, including the choreography, dancing, and supporting elements. An emotional response to any dance performance is important to acknowledge, but it is not the same as a carefully considered critique.

Questions to Consider for Evaluation

- Choreography
  - What did you notice about the way the choreographer worked with all the choreographic elements?

- Was the structure of the dance clear?
- If the title suggested a theme, did the dance follow that theme?
- Dancing of the group: The dancing of a piece of choreography is distinct from the choreography itself.
    - Do the dancers appear strong and confident?
    - Is the unison movement performed cleanly? (Note that not all choreographers strive for technical polish, and not all choreographers use unison movement.)
    - Do technically difficult sequences appear to strain the capabilities of the dancers?
    - How well are movement qualities or dramatic qualities embodied in the dancers?
    - Does the way in which the dancers move seem to complement the thrust of the choreography?
- Dancing of individuals: Are there individual dancers who stand out in the performance? If so, who are they, and why are they unique?
- Supporting elements
    - How did music, costumes, and lighting influence your perception of the piece? These supporting elements contribute to your perception of the dance as a whole. For instance, if you dislike the music for a dance, it will generally color your entire feeling for that dance.
    - Did the supporting elements work well with the concept of the dance?
    - Were they aesthetically pleasing? Why or why not?
- Opinion
    - What did you like about the dance, and why?
    - What was the most interesting thing about the dance?
    - In what ways was the dance successful or unsuccessful?

Dos and Don'ts of Evaluation

- **Support your judgments.** Building on description, analysis, and interpretation, arguments can be made to show the strengths and weaknesses of the work.

· **Use criteria appropriately.** Dances are valued for their particular expression within a genre. The features for each kind of dance are different, and so are the criteria for judging the work. For example, you would not evaluate a tap dance by the same criteria as a ballet piece.

· **Consider cultural context.** All dances are created within a cultural context. Just as it is inappropriate to evaluate tap by ballet criteria (or vice versa), it is also inappropriate to evaluate dance of one culture by the standards of another. Knowledge about a dance in its cultural context is necessary to its evaluation; if you don't have that knowledge, it is best to stick with description and analysis.

· **Understand your own biases.** Something as simple as the choreographer's choice of music can have a tremendous effect on your opinion of a work. In any evaluative process, your own personal biases or tastes will affect your feelings about a work as well as your final judgment of its strengths and weaknesses. There is really no way around this, because there is no such thing as pure objectivity. The appropriate thing to do is to acknowledge that your tastes are part of your evaluation and to be as accurate and fair as is humanly possible.

Suggested Readings for Discussing Dance

Lavender, L. 1996. *Dancers talking dance: Critical evaluation in the choreography class.* Champaign, IL: Human Kinetics

This book teaches you how to think and talk critically about student choreography in the dance composition classroom. These same skills are applicable to discussing dance performances.

Lerman, L., and J. Borstel. 2003. *Liz Lerman's critical response process.* Takoma Park, MD: Dance Exchange.

Similar to Lavender's book but with a somewhat different style, Lerman's book offers a concise approach to giving choreographic feedback, which can also be applied to talking about any dance performance.

Sklar, D. 2001. Five premises for a culturally sensitive approach to dance. In *Moving history, dancing cultures*, ed. A. Dils and A.C. Albright. Middletown, CT: Wesleyan Press.

This article offers an anthropological approach to thinking about dance, which is helpful when considering dance from a culture unfamiliar to you. The author believes that "[s]ince we all inevitably embody our own very particular cultural perspectives, we must do more than look at movement when we write about dance" (Sklar 32).

references

Adshead, Janet, ed. 1988. *Dance analysis: Theory and practice*. London: Dance Books.

American Psychological Association. 2009. Guidelines to reduce bias in language. In *Publication Manual of the American Psychological Association*. 6th ed. Washington, DC: Author.

Anderson, Jack. 1991. From Sumatra, dancing meant to be heard. *New York Times*, March 23: E3.

Asantewaa, Eva Yaa. 2008. Miguel Gutierrez and the powerful people. *Dance Magazine* April: 81-83.

Barnet, Sylvan. 2007. *A short guide to writing about art*. 9th ed. Englewood Cliffs, NJ: Prentice-Hall.

Bean, John. 1996. *Engaging ideas: The professor's guide to integrating writing, critical thinking, and active learning in the classroom*. San Francisco: Jossey-Bass.

Brown, Jean Morrison, Naomi Mindlin, and Charles Woodford. 1998. *The vision of modern dance*. 2nd ed. Hightstown, NJ: Princeton Book Company.

Bruner, Jerome. 1996. *The culture of education*. Cambridge, MA: Harvard University Press.

Bruner, Jerome. 1971. *The relevance of education*. New York: Norton.

Carter, Michael, Miriam Ferzli, and Eric Wiebe. 2007. Writing to learn by learning to write in the disciplines. *Journal of Business and Technical Communication* 21(3): 278-302.

Cohen Bull, Cynthia Jean. 1997. Sense, meaning, and perception in three dance cultures. In *Meaning in motion: New cultural studies of dance*, ed. J.C. Desmond. Durham: Duke University Press, 269-287.

Cooper, Elizabeth. 2008. Anonymous student writing samples from Cooper's advanced ballet technique class.

Elbow, Peter. 1998. *Writing without teachers*. 2nd ed. New York: Oxford University Press.

Ellis, Robert, and Charlotte Taylor. 2005. Evaluating writing instruction through an investigation of students' experiences of learning through writing. *Instructional Science* 33(1): 49-71.

Emig, Janet. May 1977. Writing as a mode of learning. *College Composition and Communication* 28: 122-28.

Feldman, Edmund. 1987. *Varieties of visual experience*. New York: Harry N. Abrams.

Fowler, H. Ramsey, and Jane E. Aaron. 1986. *The little, brown handbook*. 3rd ed. Boston: Little, Brown.

Fowler, H. Ramsey, and Jane E. Aaron. 2007. *The little, brown handbook*. 10th ed. Upper Saddle River, NJ: Longman.

Friedler, Sharon, and Susan Glazer. 1997. Dancers talk about the physical body, theory and practice and using the knowledge. In *Dancing female*, eds. Friedler and Glazer. Amsterdam: Harwood.

Gibaldi, Joseph. 1998. *MLA style manual and guide to scholarly publishing*. New York: Modern Language Association of America.

Gottschalk, Karen and Keith Hjortshoj. 2004. *The elements of teaching writing: A resource for instructors in all disciplines*. Boston: Bedford/St. Martin's Press.

Graham, Martha. 1998. Martha Graham, 1937. In *The vision of modern dance*, ed. Jean M. Brown, Naomi Mindlin, and Charles H. Woodford.

Grieg, Valerie. 1994. *Inside ballet technique*. Hightstown, NJ: Princeton Books.

Hawkins, Eric. 1967. Eric Hawkins addresses a new-to-dance audience. *Dance Magazine*, June, 42, 44.

Highwater, Jamake. 1992. *Dance: Rituals of experience*. Hightstown, NJ: Princeton Book Co.

Hilgers, Thomas, Edna Hussey, and Monica Stitt-Bergh. 1999. "As you're writing, you have these epiphanies": What college students say about writing and learning in their majors. *Written Communication* 16(3): 317-354.

Hill, Constance Valis. 2000. *Brotherhood in rhythm: The jazz tap dancing of the Nicholas Brothers*. New York: Oxford University Press.

Hirschfield, J. 1998. *Nine gates: Entering the mind of poetry.* New York: Harper Perennial.

Hodges, H.F. 1996. Journal writing as a mode of thinking for RN-BSN students: A leveled approach to learning to listen to self and others. *Journal of Nursing Education* 35(3): 137-41.

Hudson, Suzanne. 2006. *Writing about theatre & drama*. 2nd ed. Belmont, CA: Thompson Wadsworth.

Jones, Bill T. 1997. You don't have to be thin to dance. *New York Times*, July 19. OpEd.

Jowitt, Deborah. 1986. Snarls and tangles. Review of New York City Ballet. *Village Voice*, June 24. 24: 99.

Jowitt, Deborah. 1991. Joffrey Ballet. Review of Joffrey Ballet. *Village Voice*, March 19. 91: 75.

Jowitt, Deborah. 2001. Beyond description: Writing beneath the surface. In *Moving history, dancing cultures*, ed. Ann Dils and Ann C. Albright. Middletown, CT: Wesleyan Press.

Jowitt, Deborah. 2004. Perennial beauties and fresh tracks. *Village Voice*, July 28. 28: 76.

Jowitt, Deborah. 2008. Celebrating Jerome Robbins and bidding Damian Woetzel goodbye. *Village Voice*, July 2. www.villagevoice.com/content/printVersion/499436.

Kelly, L.P. 1995. Encouraging faculty to use writing as a tool to foster learning in the disciplines through writing across the curriculum. *American Annals of the Deaf* 140(1): 16-22.

Kent, Allegra. 1997. *Once a dancer* . . . New York: St. Martin's Press.

Kisselgoff, Anna. 1991. A *Giselle* celebration, from pure to romantic. Review. *New York Times*, June 7, C3.

Kraus, Richard, Sarah Hilsendager, and Brenda Dixon. 1990. Dance and the goals of contemporary education. *History of the Dance in Art and Education.* Englewood Cliffs, NJ: Prentice Hall, 303-321.

La Rocco, Claudia. 2008. Humor, seduction and a whirl of motion. *New York Times,* August 13. www.nytimes.com/2008/08/14/arts/dance/14hubb.html?ref=dance.

La Rocco, Claudia. 2008. Some noontime frolics amid the cityscape. *New York Times,* August 21. www.nytimes.com/2008/08/21/arts/dance/21dunn.html?_r=1&oref=slogin&pagewan.

Lavender, Larry. 1996. *Dancers talking dance: Critical evaluation in the choreography class.* Champaign, IL: Human Kinetics

Lerman, Liz, and John Borstel. 2003. *Liz Lerman's critical response process.* Takoma Park, MD: Dance Exchange.

Lewin, Tamar. 2003. Writing in schools is found both dismal and neglected. *New York Times,* April 26: A-15.

Looseleaf, Victoria. 2008. Is it sexist to be sexy? *Dance Magazine* (July): 44-46.

McIntosh, Peggy. 2006. White privilege: Unpacking the invisible knapsack. In *The institution of education.* 5th ed., ed. H. Shapiro, K. Latham, and S. Ross. Boston: Pearson, pp. 238-242.

Meltzer, Irene. 1979. The critical eye: An analysis of the process of dance criticism as practiced by Clive Barnes, Arlene Croce, Deborah Jowitt, Elizabeth Kendall, Marcia Siegel, and David Vaughn. Master's thesis, Ohio State University.

Miller, Casey, and Kate Swift. 1976. *Words and women.* Garden City, NY: Anchor Press/Doubleday.

Morgenroth, Joyce. 2004. *Speaking of dance: Twelve contemporary choreographers on their craft.* New York: Routledge.

National Commission on Writing in America's Schools and Colleges. 2003. *The neglected "R": The need for a writing revolution.* Report. College Entrance Examination Board.

National Dance Education Organization. 2005. *Standards for learning and teaching dance in the arts: Ages 5-18.* Bethesda, MD: National Dance Education Organization. www.ndeo.org/content.aspx?page_id=22&club_id=893257&module_id=55412.

Northrop, F.S.C. 1946. *The meeting of east and west: An inquiry concerning world understanding.* New York: MacMillan.

Novak, Cynthia. 1990. *Sharing the dance: Contact improvisation and American culture.* Madison, WI: University of Wisconsin Press.

Oliver, Wendy. 1991. Interview by Elizabeth Zimmer (dance critic). August 10. New York.

Oxbrow, Gina. 2005. Writing, reflection and learning—an interactive approach. *Porta Linguarum* 4: 167-84.

Pabon, Jorge Fabel. 2008. Foundations of hip-hop dance. *Dance and culture: An introductory reader,* ed. Wendy Oliver. Reston, VA: National Dance Association, 59-61.

Perron, Wendy. 2008. Festival Ballet Providence. *Dance Magazine,* April: 80-81. New York: McFadden Performing Arts Media.

Quitadamo, Ian, and Martha Kurtz. 2007. Learning to improve: Using writing to increase critical thinking performance in general education biology. *Life Sciences Education* 6: 140-154.

Rhode Island and New Hampshire Local Grade Level & Grade Span Expectations for Written and Oral Communication including New England Common Assessment Program, State Grade Level and Grade Span Expectations for Writing. 2006. http://www.ride.ri.gov/Instruction/DOCS/gle/GLE%20pdf/FINAL/Grades%20K-5%20Written%20and%20Oral%20Comm%20%20GLEs%20Final%20Version%202006.pdf.

Rivard, Leonard P., and Stanley B. Straw. 2000. The effect of talk and writing on learning science: An exploratory study. *Science Education* 84 (5): 566.

Sandler, Julie. 1997. Standing in awe, sitting in judgment. *Dancing female,* eds. Friedler and Glazer. Amsterdam: Harwood.

Sharples, Mike, and S. Ransdell, eds. 1996. An account of writing as creative design. In *The science of writing: Theories, methods, individual differences, and applications.* Mahwah, NJ: Lawrence Erlbaum Associates.

Siegel, Marcia. 1976. *Watching the dance go by.* Boston: Houghton-Mifflin.

Sklar, Deirdre. 2001. Five premises for a culturally sensitive approach to dance. In *Moving history, dancing cultures,* ed. A. Dils and A.C. Albright. Middletown, CT: Wesleyan Press.

Strunk, William, and E.B. White. 2008. *The elements of style.* Upper Saddle River, NJ: Longman.

Supree, Burt. 1991. Elizabeth Streb ringside. Review. *The Village Voice,* June 4.

Taylor, Paul. 1999. *Private domain.* Pittsburgh: University of Pittsburgh Press.

Thaiss, Christopher, and Rick Davis. 1999. *Writing about theatre.* Needham Heights, MA: Allyn and Bacon.

Tobias, Tobi. 2004. Heidi Latsky's latest show teeters between club and concert dancing. Review. *The Village Voice,* July 28.

University of Chicago. 2003. *Chicago manual of style.* 15th ed. Chicago: Author.

Vasilyuk, Sasha. 2007. Review: Mozart Dances is supremely musical. *San Francisco Examiner,* September 21. www.sfexaminer.com/entertainment/review_mozart_dances_is_supremely_musical2.

Webb, Norman. 2005. TILSA alignment tool. PowerPoint presentation. http://wat.wceruw.org.

Webb, Norman. 2007. Issues related to judging the alignment of curriculum standards and assessments. *Applied Measurement in Education* 20.1: 7-25.

Webb, Norman, et al. 2006. Web alignment tool. Wisconsin Center of Educational Research, University of Wisconsin at Madison. www.wcer.wisc.edu/WAT/index.aspx.

index

Note: The italicized *f* and *t* following page numbers refer to figures and tables, respectively.

about the author

Wendy Oliver, **EdD,** is a professor of dance in the department of theater, dance, and film at Providence College in Providence, Rhode Island. She has degrees in English (bachelor's degree from Grinnell College), dance (master's degree from Temple University), and dance education (EdD from Columbia University) and has taught dance at the college level for over 20 years. She believes that writing has a place in every dance course and she incorporates dance criticism, dance research, and informal dance writing into her classes on a regular basis.

Oliver worked briefly as a dance critic, and later wrote her dissertation on the teaching of dance criticism at the college level. She has edited three books, and has published dance articles in a variety of books and journals, including the *Journal of Dance in Education; Dance Research Journal;* and the *Journal of Physical Education, Recreation, and Dance.* She is an editorial board member for the *Journal of Dance in Education* and has served on the board for the Congress on Research for Dance. She also served as director of publications for the National Dance Association and is co-coordinator of the Rhode Island Arts Proficiencies in Dance.

Oliver was honored in *Who's Who of American Women* in 2008 to 2009 and received the National Dance Association Scholar/Artist Award in 2008. She was also listed in *Who's Who Among America's Teachers* from 2003 to 2006 and received the Dance Educator of the Year Award in 1998 from the Rhode Island AAHPERD.

You'll find other outstanding
dance resources at
www.HumanKinetics.com